Divas Delight

by:

j. toby mckinney

Divas Delight
Copyright © 2012

First Printing, InkWell Press, USA 2012

Library of Congress Cataloging-in-Publication Data

ISBN 978-0615585819
ISBN-0615585817

While on this earth we often go through many trials and tribulations. But if not for the help, love, care and support from friends and loved ones, we would surely perish. I want to thank the many people who have been there through this journey of life with me:

Kim: We've gone through a lot together; both individually and as friends, throughout the course of our lives. Our life-long friendship has withstood the test of time, and is a testament as to the depth and breadth true friendship can span. Thanks for giving me my *VERY OWN* "Will & Grace/ Sex and the City" experience! I am forever grateful for having known you, having you as a "sister-girlfriend", and for our recent discovery that; after all these years of knowing each other…we are ***actually*** related! How cool is that??? I will always cherish the unique and exquisite "BGF" friendship that we have. *Thank you, cuz!!!!*

Marchae', Dayna and Kayla: Thank you for your continued love and support; and for allowing me to be there for you to show you the uncle I'd always known I could be to you guys.

Jay/Beth and "the kids": Thanks to your continued love and support. Look forward to what's in store for us next.

Don: Persistence has paid off! I am so glad to *finally* have you back in my life! These past several years have just seemed to melt away; and it's as if we're back where we left off. Thank you for your continued patience, guidance, strength and support; and for keeping me safe and sane during this project. Your abundance of friendship and love hasn't gone unnoticed.

Earl: What can I say that I haven't already said before? I can't tell you how much your continued friendship means to me. We've gone through a lot together, I am truly thankful that you're still in my life.

Mark, Art, Tonyo, Chris H, Ellyce, Jeff H, The
Brothers of Kappa Psi Kappa Fraternity, Inc.,
and to all of my friends from Grambling State
University, USAF, in both Pittsburgh and Ft.
Lauderdale, and from the different jobs I've
worked in: you *all* have touched my life in one
way or another. There are many of you that I am
still trying to get back in touch with. For those of
you that I have been able to locate and re-
establish correspondence with; thanks for
allowing me back into your lives.

To everyone at CreateSpace and InkWell
Press:

A heartfelt thanks goes out to you for all of your
assistance in helping me get my project
completed.

This book is dedicated to the family, friends and mentors who have come into my life, but have "gone too soon". It is for these people that I put my words to paper. They have inspired and encouraged me to tell my stories; so that they can live on forever, even once *I'm* gone. I know that you guys would all be so proud of me and my successes. I miss you all very deeply:

In Memory of:

My mentor, E. Lynn Harris, Theodore Williams, Teddy Williams, Saul White, David Willems, Gene Williams, Reed Madden, Lamont Arnold, Robert Bailey, Terrell Pickett, George Benson, Jr., Stuart Smiley, David Buccilli, Bill "Untugu" Robinson; Reggie Johnson, Dwight Fullum,

Donald McDaniels, Jim Michaud, Dean Miller,
Thommie Williamson, Bill Weber, Dellmarr Jones,
Robert Bailey, Dwight Fullum, Reed Madden,
Roland House, Lamar Frazier, Herman McClain,
Sylvia Woodson, and as always; most
importantly to my grandparents-James &
Penelope Jones

~j. toby mckinney

Chapter One

*A*s she sat there alone; just the glowing embers of her cigarette to help illuminate the darkness, she allowed her body to succumb to the effects of the glass of warm cognac that she was nursing. Her mind began to drift and wander back over the circumstances that led her to this point in her life; events that impacted her future. Every sinew of her toned, supple and lithe body was now glistening with sweat beads as she pondered her next move. Why had she not seen all of the tell-tale signs that had lead up to that fateful night? How many of her "friend-girls" warned her that she was living in a fantasy land; that her marriage; (and husband for that matter), was not as perfect as she wanted it to be. No one's was; but Bianca swore, because deep in her mind she thought it so, that hers was the exception. She swore to herself; though, that she was *not* going to be like a lot of women who turn a blind eye while their men are out "messin'" with" anything that walks by; male *or* female. She knew that she was not going to be played.

By all accounts, Bianca had it all: a loving husband, her own stash of money in the bank, a wonderful nest egg for when they retired, a beautiful mini-manse in the Toney, exclusive, all-white section of Parkland in Ft. Lauderdale, vacationed all over the world, completed with several summer homes. Yes, by all accounts Bianca Paxton-Malloy had arrived. Never mind that the road was paved with regrets, recriminations, deceit, and a *teeeensy* bit of whoring thrown in; but hell,
who doesn't have a few skeletons in their closet these days? Lord knows that her childhood idols

have all let her down by having scandalous pasts, so why should she be any different. She had made good on the vow she made to herself when she was a little girl growing up on her grandmother's tenement farm back in Louisiana. Only then she was known as Beulah Mae Patterson, a fairly attractive girl living in a shit-hole town called Houma, Louisiana. There was nothing much to talk about Houma; and most of the residents couldn't wait to grow up and get the hell away from it; including Beulah Mae.

Her grandmother for whom she was named after; Beulah, was a hard working, God-fearing, no nonsense kind of woman. She was charged with raising young Beulah Mae when her mother left her there one weekend. She just never came back for her. A few months later there was a telegram all the way from Paris, France. Gladys Ann had left her daughter in the care of her grandmother to run off with some traveling burlesque show, and had ended up as a chorus girl in one of the off-stage productions of the

Follies-Bérgère. Beulah was infuriated! Hadn't she taught her daughter better than that; than to run off and leave her only offspring to be cared by her own mother? Beulah couldn't bear to tell the community or her church-going friends the truth, so she did what she had to do to protect her new charge. She told everyone that her daughter had decided to mend her ways of "drinking and cattin' about"; left young Beulah Mae with her and was doing missionary work over in Ghana, Africa. The only way she knew anything about Ghana was that she had heard it early one morning while her radio was recounting the latest missionary and revival events that were going on. Beulah did not own any modern convenience except a radio. She was too proud of a woman to accept hand-me-downs, and felt that television was the work of the devil. She accepted radio, but only listened when her favorite pastors were on the air on Sunday evenings, as she was winding down her Sunday chores.

Beulah Mae Floyd and her husband; the late Earl Floyd, were plain, simple, ordinary folk. When Earl was alive, they worked together as farmers, using the little bit of land that they owned to grow and sell fresh produce to some of the local general stores in the three-parish area. Beulah supplemented their income by working part-time as a cleaning lady for some of the businessmen that owned businesses in and around Houma. Since the Floyds didn't own a car, Beulah was limited to how far she could travel, as none of the white businessmen would be seen dead having a "cullah-ed woman" riding around in their cars. Beulah didn't mind the walk; it gave her more time to practice her hymns and bible recitals for Sunday service. Lord knows; when she got home, she wouldn't have a moment to herself with all the raucous her brood unleashed on her as she rounded the dirt walkway leading to their farm. The Floyd farm was not really a farm at all; just a small, two story, two bedroom A-frame house that the whole family maintained to the best of their abilities. Since the boys were learning on-the-job trades, and were able to haul away anything that they could salvage from the work sites they did, they were able to patch things up and keep the house moderately together. But as the boys got older and began to see less and less work being tossed their way; they grew tired and weary of the sleepy little town and moved away, leaving Beulah and Earl there to tend to the repairs themselves. The house really fell into shambles once Earl suffered his stroke and was no longer ambulatory. The doctor had told Earl many years earlier that he needed to slow down; that his heart was not going to be able to hold up unless he took it easy, but how could he? There was just so much that he had to do to keep a roof over his family's head, and he still had his wife and four of his eleven children at home to be cared for. Thank God that he died peacefully in his sleep the night his last child; Gladys Ann, said her good-byes as she became a young bride to

Caleb Patterson; she was only fifteen, he was seventeen.

Caleb took one of the other ways out of Houma; he joined the military. Caleb was, by no means, a stellar student in school. He struggled desperately to stay afloat and make it to the ninth grade. He had been held back both in the second and sixth, and so he knew that it was only a matter of time before he was going to be held back again, so he got his parents to sign him out and he joined the Army. After basic training, Caleb was shipped directly to the front lines in Laos; as this was the height of the Vietnam War, and Caleb was ready to see some of the world he had known nothing about, but had only heard about through church and the little schooling he did attend. At first; the letters Gladys received were glamorous and exciting. She couldn't wait to pack her bags and be whisked off to Laos and dress in that strange white make-up she had seen so many times in the travel magazines that her mother often brought home. She wanted to wear those dresses with the purses in the back that were made out of fancy silk material, and walk around holding an umbrella, even when it was sunny outside. But she was absolutely dying to try on those wooden high heels that she always saw them wear. She didn't quite understand why they were on two wooden slats, where here in America, it was just one spiked heel, but she swore that she would learn. She had asked several of the men that she knew around town what the name of "those ladies" were called, and she had been told they were "Geechies" or "Gayshees". All she knew was that she wanted to learn to dress like one. She wanted to be slathered in make-up, silks, little jingly things sticking out of her hair, she wanted it all and Caleb was going to be her means to provide it.

Caleb was unsure as to what his new wife thought about the job that he did. She obviously didn't know that he was over there to kill other people; all she wanted to know was when he was going to buy her some of those silky robes she saw. She constantly sent him pictures from magazines with different kimonos circled with notes: "Buy me two-no three- of these"; and requests for some stupid wooden high heels. No matter how many times he told her he didn't have time to shop, she would get angry and tell him that he didn't love her. How could he; they were married on a Saturday, and Monday morning he shipped out to Boot Camp? There was no time for a honeymoon; they barely even knew each other. Yes, he vaguely knew of her from what his mother had been telling him, but for Caleb, Gladys was too young. Fifteen was way too young for him to consider a wife; hell, she was just beginning to develop breasts. But he finally conceded after his father and uncles were able to convince him that his current girlfriend, Grace Jeters, was pregnant by Willie Josephs, the only son of Houma's Chief of Police; the bigoted *white* Chief of Police. They convinced Caleb to hurry up and marry Gladys before Chief Josephs found out that she was pregnant and would be looking to pin it on him. It would take a while before the truth would come to light, but by that time, Caleb would probably have been pushing up daisies out in Ezra's field; where poor folks get buried without coffins so that their bodies decompose right into the soil as fertilizer for Mr. Ezra's cows to graze on the grass.

Growing up; Bianca had always suffered with low self-esteem. Instead of relishing in her model-esque body; (as a teenager, she was constantly being compared to the young Diana Ross). But Bianca saw nothing attractive with a body that had about as much femininity as a pre-pubescent boy. While all of her other female classmates were relishing in getting stares at their newly developed breasts and feminine curves, Bianca's body simply refused to take shape. She also detested the fact that she was one of the darkest people in her community. It was unfortunate that she was not comfortable in her own skin tone. She had inherited her family's genes of having the most evenly toned, unblemished cocoa brown complexion; the kind that needs a liberal amount of makeup in order to enhance its beauty. This lack of self assurance led Bianca to subject herself to the "old wives' tales" to "enhance" her body to its current perfection. She took great pains to keep up with ever-changing fashion trends by keeping it toned and buffed. Her diligence paid off; she married the first man that asked her; the first one who ever showed any hint of interest towards her.

How she longed to go back to that moment in time knowing all that she knows now. She would have saved herself this pain and anguish by waiting a bit longer for another prospect. Bianca was now immersed in the task of building her dream home like Fay Dunaway did in "Mommie Dearest". She was there; every day, barking orders and firing people who didn't do it *exactly* the way she wanted it. Caleb could have gave a damn less; to him, it was *her* house. He just signed the checks; never asked to see any bills, never asked any questions. She told him the day they were going to move in; he arranged for the moving van. If only she realized then that his laissez-faire attitude would someday prove to be a much bigger issue and have a much greater impact in their relationship...

Chapter Two

Charmaine Porter was the group's bombshell; she was a definite knockout. She was voluptuous, curvaceous, flirty, and used her feminine wiles to get whatever she wanted out of life. She never had time for marriage, thought it tied her down, and after all that Charmaine had been through growing up, she wanted no parts of being tied down to a man. Her step-father; the late Rev. Dr. Jimmy Porter, in his heyday had the single-most largest congregation in West Memphis, Arkansas. The good Reverend had fancied himself to be the next Rev. Dr. Martin Luther King, Jr. There was one slight flaw in Reverend Porter's character that he kept a secret; a secret that shattered his family and destroyed his relationship with his youngest daughter, Charmaine, forever.

Charmaine didn't find it easy making many female friends; since she oozed sexuality, she was

often branded a "home wrecker". The one thing
that she wanted desperately was to find friends;
hell, even *one* friend, that wasn't afraid of her
woman-ness. Until she met her "girls",
Charmaine thought she was going to go through
this life without someone to lean on, someone to
share her *sameness* with. At first, she was
reticent; aloof, guarded. It wasn't until she met
the other three women that fateful day in the real
estate office that she felt she finally found people
who could possibly hold their own against her.
By the time they all closed on their respective
houses; they were fast friends. She was the last
of the bunch to close; not because hers was the
hardest; it was predominately due to the fact that
the demands of her job constantly made her
keep holding off from signing the paperwork.
Charmaine was a lawyer assigned to the Family
Court division; she split her time between
Domestic Court and working pro bono for the
local Women's Domestic Abuse shelter. Initially;

she looked at it as a punishment for being so sensual, but as she really got involved with her clients; really got to know them personally, she began to take her job to heart and see that she had a way to directly impact their lives. She made herself available to them whenever they were in need; sometimes putting her own self at risk against the abusive partner.

Charmaine soon made a name for herself. There was no where she could go in Broward County without a Sheriff's Deputy, Police Officer, or even ordinary people on the street stopping her to chat. They really appreciated the fact that she was visible in the community; whenever there was a major function being held in one of the county-run parks she was there, eating the soul food plates that people made for her, speaking about women's issues and issues of domestic violence, helping out with the kids by organizing games or reading to the young tikes. She regularly attended church in the communities; making the rounds from community church to community church so that every pastor got to know her and recognize her when she entered through the doors. This in and of itself was hard for Charmaine; given the hell that she had been through with her father, but she said a prayer each and every time and made sure that she had a flask of her momma's homemade "tonic" to help her get past the demons that haunted her.

For Charmaine, it was easier for her not to belong to any one congregation. She was able to effortlessly float in and out of services without really being missed too much by the elders of the church. Many a pastor had tried to get her to commit to his (or her) church; but Charmaine always tells them that she prefers to "spread the wealth throughout the community". But the true fact of the matter is that Charmaine has not been able to reconcile within herself the pain and anger she has been harboring all these years towards her father for robbing her of her youth; for saddling her with the knowledge of womanhood before her time. Deep in her heart she knew that there was going to come a time when she was going to have to confront her father; to get him to admit publicly what he had done to her; and suffer the consequences of his actions, She was not going to be whole again until this was done. She could only hide her shame and guilt for so long before it began to eat away at the very core of her being. She was slowly coming to that point, but was staving it off by placing work, friends, and now a new home in its path. But it was *not* going to be ignored; it was coming to the surface…and fast! And try as she might; Charmaine was incapable of stopping it, she had no advance warning of where or when it was going to creep up on her, for she was pushing herself so as to ignore it. But it was going to have its say…

Chapter Three

*A*llison Taylor was the one born into the black elite bourgeois aristocracy. She was the only child of Senator Mildred and Ezra Taylor, from Augusta, Georgia. Allison had every luxury in life she could have ever wanted. She attended only the finest upper-crust finishing school that her parents' money could buy; partly because they didn't want for Allison to know that their marriage was a sham. Ezra had been a philanderer all of his life. He had married Mildred in order to save face when his own parents caught him in bed with the daughter of one of his father's rival white business associates. Ezra had been attracted not only to women, but specifically to *white* women, for as long as he could remember. He tried as hard as he could to feign disdain for them as a front for his father's sake. But he had always yearned that someday, his family could accept the fact that he happened to have a white wife;

but he knew that it was an impossibility.

Mildred had gotten herself "in the family way" with a ne'er-do-well drifter that was in town for the Mardi Gras festivities. In order to save face, Mildred's father secretly paid Ezra's father a dowry; and ensured that Mildred would be of no trouble to him, if Ezra would agree to marry her. Neither Ezra nor Mildred were in any particular position to object; so, they both put on their game faces and did what they had to do. By all accounts; their lives seemed picture perfect to the outside world. They had carefully spelled out the ground rules out as to how their marriage was to be. And as long as both of them stuck to the arrangement, what they did with their own private lives was neither of the other one's concern.

As far as their daughters were concerned; nothing in their lives seemed a bit out of place, Ezra and Mildred saw to it that nothing was. But the interesting thing about keeping secrets and lies; especially in the political arena, is that somehow...someway... things seem to get brought to light that one may not particularly be ready for. Ezra had dodged several bullets in his career. There had been many congressional interns who had brought charges of behavioral misconduct and sexual harassment against him. Since he had made many political allies who helped get the charges squashed and kept out of the papers.

   For her part, Mildred always looked the other way as she stood by her man. No matter how many times she had been confronted with the allegations; she rebuffed them, even though she knew in her heart of hearts that he probably did what he was accused of. She would never bring any of this up to Ezra; why should she? He kept her in the lifestyle she had always aspired to. No one could have planned on the chain of events that would send Ezra's career plummeting to the ground. Up to this point in his career, Ezra watched as his colleagues' careers took major hits. It all came to a head during the time of

President Bill Clinton's "Lewinsky" fiasco. Shortly after President's affair came to the surface; many other politicians found themselves being investigated for "dalliances". The Ken Starr/Linda Tripp machine was in full swing; and was taking no prisoners.

One of its final casualties happened to be Ezra Taylor. It all started out like a seemingly innocent courier delivery. As usual; Ezra's secretary contacted him, informing her that the package was addressed to Mildred directly and marked "urgent". When Mildred opened the package; she was shocked and appalled. There; in her hand, was documented proof of her husband's sexual proclivities. Mildred tried; with all her might, to turn away. Curiosity got the best of her, and she felt that she *had* to look; no matter how bad it was. With each subsequent photo, Mildred felt the knot in her stomach tighten. When she was done looking at the photos, Mildred went to place them back in the envelope when she found a note that was included. The note informed

Mildred that copies of the photos had also been delivered to the news agencies; both local and national, and were also being posted on the internet. Mildred's mind began to swim.

   She knew that Ezra was in for a long, drawn out battle with the pundits and paparazzi. Mildred had to steel herself for what was about to come, for it was going to get ugly pretty quickly. Her next thought was whether or not to contact Ezra and give him the "head's-up" as to what was about to be coming down the pike. On the one hand; she felt a certain sense of duty; her being his wife and all. On the other hand; she was tired of all the political bullshit that she had been forced to put up with. She wanted nothing more than for Ezra's political career to be over, so that she could leave him and move on with her life. Ezra could finally have the relationships with his "women"; out in the open, as a private citizen. She decided to "let the chips fall where they may"; so to speak. She realized that she was given the leverage that she needed to force

Ezra's hand. With the impending "smear campaign" that was about to ensue, she figured she would gain the sympathy of his constituents when she announced that she was filing for divorce. Mildred knew that she was holding the "smoking gun" in her hand. The only thing she had to do now was to find someplace safe to keep it where Ezra (or anyone else; for that matter), was sure not to find it.

   She didn't have much time to think, before the telephone rang. When her assistant came into the room and told her that Ezra was on the other line, she instinctively knew that he had already been contacted.

"Hello…?" she said; as if she was unsure who was on the other end.

"Millie; it's Ezz…; has anyone been by the house today to drop off a package?" He asked; with a certain sense of urgency in his voice.

"Not that I know of; let me ask Anna."   Mildred put the phone down; went to the door and called her personal assistant; Anna. She made sure that Ezra overheard her speaking to Anna; but in a voice just barely enough to sound above a whisper. She made sure that Ezra heard her dismiss Anna as she made her way back to the phone.

"No; nothing has come yet. Anna said that she would have put it in your desk chair if it had. Do you want me to let you know when it arrives?" She asked, coyly.

"Yeah; call me as soon as it arrives, and I'll have someone come over and pick it up." Ezra replied. A broad grin crept across Mildred's face as she replaced the receiver on its cradle. She knew that the ball was now in her court. She then turned her attention to finding a temporary hiding place for the package until a more advantageous one could be located. She figured that she'd have enough time before he got home to put it away...she was wrong. She heard the engine of Ezra's car as it made its way down the driveway.

"Shit!" she mumbled to herself; as she

scrambled about the room, frantic.

She scurried into the bathroom; where she closed and locked the door behind her. She knew that she had to take another shower in order to muffle the sounds of her rooting around in there. As she was about to step into the shower; her eye caught a glimpse of the perfect hiding place. She tore over to the clothes hamper, and dumped everything onto the floor. She placed the envelope down on the bottom of the hamper, and replaced the clothes back on top of it. She jumped into the shower, and quickly washed herself off. This also bought her some time to come up with her next move.

When she exited the shower; she feigned to be startled by Ezra's presence. As she made her way over to her vanity to dry herself off. Ezra sat in the overstuffed chair that was at the other end of the room; nursing what appeared to be a stiff drink. "Jeezus...Ezra; you scared the daylights out of me!" Mildred shrieked; as she dropped her towel for effect. "What are you doing here so early?" She had to contain her emotions in her voice. She didn't want to give anything away.

"Get dressed; I wanna take you out to dinner tonight." Ezra said.

"Now?" Mildred said as she searched the room; looking for some sort of clock.

"Yeah; now…We can drive out to the country; out to that little inn that you like so much". Ezra replied.

"Ezra…you know how *long* that drive is going to take, out there and back?" Mildred knew that Ezra knew she had him. "So; what gives? Why you wanna drive out there at this time of night?" She said; as she began to approach him. She was now putting on her robe. She let him off the hook…for now.

"Sure; why not? Let's go!" She said; as she slapped herself on the thigh. She spun around and headed towards her closet. Ezra pulled himself out of the chair and headed over towards her. He pulled her body close to his; and nestled his chin in the crook of her neck.

"Thanks; Millie...I appreciate this more than you'll ever know".

Mildred turned around and looked up at Ezra; square in his face.

"What's going on; Ezz...?" She asked.

"I just need to get away; far...far away from here just for tonight". Ezra said softly.

For a brief, fleeting moment Mildred wanted to sit Ezra down and tell him what she knew. It had been a long time; actually... never, that she had ever seen him break down and be vulnerable with her. She felt sorry for him. Then; she remembered the photos, and was instantly reviled.

She knew that she could not let him off the hook. He was about to drag her through and the girls' good name through the mud. She knew that they didn't deserve what was about to happen to them; yet they had no other recourse but to survive the onslaught that they were about to endure. Mildred wanted to just push him away and cuss his ass up one side and down the other. Her first mind was to shove the pictures in his face and make him explain to her what the fuck was going on. But her second mind won out; and she continued to play it cool and see what line of shit Ezra was going to try and feed her *this* time.

.

Chapter Four

 Leslie Scott was the one with the heart of gold. It was too bad that she believed in and fell in love with every no-good-low-life that had some sort of checkered history. For all of her good looks, Leslie was the most insecure of the bunch. She had no particular reason for it, her upbringing was as normal and as close to picture-perfect as could be. There wasn't much to tell about the Scott family; Mr. Alvin and Mrs. Cora-Lee Scott were solid, decent hard working people from St. Louis, Missouri. They raised their two daughters, Catherine and Leslie, as salt of the earth, upstanding members of the community. They raised them with as much Christian values and sent them out into the world on their own with the knowledge that they had armed their girls with a good sense of what was right and wrong. They provided them handsomely while they were attending their college of choice, Catherine, the oldest, chose to attend Howard University and went on to become "Miss Black America" her final year in Grad school. She is now one of the leading Black female gynecologists in the Baltimore area. Leslie, chose to matriculate at the University of Miami, and completed her Master's in Public Health. She is currently the head of the Infectious Disease Division of the Broward County Health Department. Leslie met and fell head over heels in love with a bright, articulate strikingly drop-dead hunk of an intern at the free clinic; Peter Naylor. They were engaged to be married; and the wedding was planned for the spring, before the weather became too unbearable.

Peter's upbringing was parallel to Leslie's. He grew up in the all-black enclave of Omaha, Nebraska. He was the captain of his high school football team; and went on to be a star player at the University of Nebraska. He was picked up as a third-string player for the Kansas City Chiefs; and was in his fourth year of his five year contract. He wasn't sure whether or not he was going to be picked up again; or be traded to another team. Up to this point; Peter hadn't played a single game with the Chiefs. He knew that he had to pay his dues; and he was willing. Things were now at a crucial stage between he and Leslie; and his career was now in limbo. He knew that once they got married; Leslie would give up her job and follow his career as a football wife. The thing about his theory is that he had never discussed any of it with *her*. It wasn't that he didn't care about her or her desires; he was just an old-fashioned guy, and believed that once he was the primary breadwinner of the family that his new wife had no reason to work again.

Leslie was a bit more level-headed and realistic. She knew that there was the possibility that Peter's football career was over. He had spent four years on the bench; and in her mind, no team was not going to spend money on a player who had never stepped foot on the field. Leslie was unaware of Peter's beliefs about marriage. As far as she was concerned; it never even crossed her mind that she would have to give up her career; the career that she had worked so hard to achieve. Leslie felt sure that she could see the handwriting on the wall; that Peter was going to be "washed up" once his contract expired. She had been trying to get him to pursue other ventures while he was still making the money that he was; but every time she would bring it up, he would put her off. Leslie was getting a bit agitated that he was basing their future on the possibility that may or may not happen. She just couldn't understand why this football career was so tantamount in Peter's life.

It was becoming increasingly clear to Leslie that maybe she should consider someone else as a mate. She wasn't sure whether or not she was truly being fair to Peter. She tried to bring it up to both her parents and Peter's. Her mother and father seemed to be able to weigh both sides of the story. Peter's parents; however, were not as open minded. She began to see what the motivating factor was as to why Peter was so adamant on making it big in the NFL. It was his father's failed dream. Leslie knew that there was no way that she was ever going to be able to get his parents to see the fact that Peter may never play professional football. It was not in their vocabulary to say "quit". Leslie's big fear was that Peter was chasing a dream that wasn't necessarily his; and feared that he was going to be devastated when he realized that his prospects for another chance on another team were next to none. She also was concerned as to how Mr. Naylor was going to view Peter if he doesn't make another team. She felt a bit overwhelmed by all of this; which only made her doubts grow even greater. She really began to re-evaluate her stance on the relationship.

Chapter Five

Of the five girls, Brenda "Bee Bee" Gaines was the ditzy one. Not so much that she was truly ditzy, but she was the one that was the most "country". Try as she might, she just couldn't let go of her small town mentality. Bee Bee was the group's version of Sinclair from the hit sitcom "Living Single"; in fact, the other girls had dubbed her "Sinclair". She was raised similarly to Bianca; a matronly spinster Aunt took her mother in when she had gotten pregnant with Brenda up in her home town of Belle Glades, just a few miles north of Ft. Lauderdale. Belle Glades was one of the poorer sections of Palm Beach County; inhabited mainly by dirt poor blacks and immigrant Mexicans working in the sugar cane fields. Belle Glades had one of the largest concentrations of section-8 government tract-style complexes still left in Florida. Clara and Brenda lived together in a one-bedroom home, with Brenda sleeping on a cot in her Aunt's bedroom. Since quarters were so cramped, and Brenda was but and infant, Clara was able to care for Brenda with little disruption in her life at this time as possible. Clara delighted in the fact that the Good Lord had blessed her with Brenda; and she was going to do everything in her power to make sure that Brenda had a chance at a better life than she had. Brenda's home was one of the more upscale ones in the neighborhood. Since Clara was working as a nurse at the local free clinic, she made considerably more than the rest of her neighbors. She had decided when she took the job, going on some twenty plus years ago, that since it was only she that she had to provide for, she wasn't going to waste good money on overpriced housing; she was going to by a small, yet moderately priced home and save the rest of her money for her golden years. With any salary increases and bonuses she ever earned, she would use them to travel with. By all accounts, Clara lived very frugally. Even when Brenda came into her life, she readily took donations of clothing and baby supplies from whoever was willing to donate them to her.

Brenda began dating a man, Chad Has lip. He was not what anyone would call "drop-dead gorgeous"; but he had that certain *look* about him. He gave you the impression that you had seen him in some sort of advertisement before, but you just weren't sure for exactly which product or magazine you saw him in. He had all of the classic features of a model; the chiseled jawline, the washboard abs and just the right amount of muscle on his biceps so that he didn't look "bulky". You could tell that he had spent a fortune on his teeth; they were absolutely flawless, and he must have stayed on the beach in order to have that constant tanned look. With all of that "perfection", he did have a couple of flaws; which they all do. The first one that was unnoticeable when you first met him was that he was partially blind. His quest for vanity came at a huge cost to his health. When he had just started out in his modeling career, he had flown down to Mexico to have an operation which was supposed to be able to change his eye color. Chad was told that the Doctor was able to make his eyes any color that he wanted with a new procedure he had developed using lasers. Chad plopped down his five thousand dollars and flew into Acapulco for the weekend operation. Not only did it *not* change his eye color, but the damage that was done to his eyesight was irreparable. He had to wear thick glasses in order to see, but he was too vain to use them. He was able to make out distinguishable shapes, and when on photo shoots, his camera man knew how to use verbal cues to get him in the right angle for the shots. That is why he was not able to make the big money doing runway modeling; he had taken a few tumbles and decided it was not worth him putting his life in danger. But the biggest flaw Brenda found out during one of their dates.

She and Chad had begun getting serious. He

had wined and dined her and he attributed his nearsightedness and sensitivity to light to all of the bright lights and direct sunlight he had been exposed to all of his career. When things started to heat up back at his condo off of Collins Avenue down on South Beach, Brenda thought she had hit pay dirt! She could never have imagined; in her wildest dreams, an apartment this expanse, this opulent, this...magnificent! Every wall had some rare one-of-a-kind object that just took your breath away. There was a gallery of artwork; with names such as Warhol, Haring, Bearden, Lieberman, and Hirschfield. Brenda was captivated by all of the pictures that adorned every available space imaginable: Him with such celebs as the original Broadway cast of "Dreamgirls"; a' la Jennifer Holliday, local anchorman Craig Stevens and weatherman Bill Kamal, numerous backstage pictures featuring him and Cher, Madonna, Diana, Whitney, Luther, Patti, Mariah, Anita, Gloria, Barbra, Grace (Jones-not Slick); along with several others that suggested that he had traveled around the world. What captured Brenda's attention most was the extensive collection of pictures he had with groups of men. Men she had never seen before, but were signed with some sort of cryptic messages. She studied the wordings and committed them to memory so that she could ask "the girls" to see if any of them knew what they meant.

By the time the evening wore on; Brenda had put aside her inquiry into the pictures; especially after she discovered that Chad had started out as an underwear model for AmariMen; an exclusive men's underwear off-shoot of International Male. Chad was all too eager to show her the ads that launched his career. He was modeling part-time while he was making ends meet as a fledgling flight attendant for People's Express Airlines. Chad had been with them from the start; through the bankruptcy, and had managed to work his way through the airline industry until he landed a cushy position with JetBlue. That began to explain all of the exotic locations he was able to be in; and why his artwork was something that you just didn't see everyday. He told Brenda that he was able to meet tons of celebrities over the years. Brenda then asked him what the "Falcon Club" was. Chad; never skipping a beat, told her that it was a group of male flight attendants that he belonged to, a sort of clique that hung together and partied whenever they all got together. Brenda's uneasiness was laid to rest. Chad told her that he played down his profession; didn't like to brag about it, it was a job just like any other. He was able to work part-time at both, doing what he loved and flexing his schedule when it was convenient for him; not them. He told her that he often would get interrupted by his agent with assignments to fly to exotic locations for shoots, but assured her that he would not let that get in their way whenever they were together. He had already informed him ahead of time, so that the answering machine would get it and they didn't have to be disturbed.

Brenda was lulled into a false sense of security by Chad. She had no way of knowing that he was deceiving her. But as her auntie always used to say; "Be careful what you do in the darkness, for it will always come to light". She never really quite understood what she had meant by that; she was soon going to learn…but good!

Chapter Six

Leslie was so excited about the prospect of getting married. She knew that she was ready. She had always wanted the white picket fence and 2.2 children with the station wagon and Old English Sheepdog as a family pet. Leslie wanted the same thing that she saw her parents have. She didn't realize that times were different than when they first got together. The world had turned narcissistic and self-centered. It was now in the "ME-ME-ME" generation; with all of the glut of dot com-ers that were flooding the economy with excessive spending and instant gratification "toys". So many of her family and friends were driving around in Lexuses; Jags, Benzes, BMW's; she had lost count. She; too, had been tempted to study computer science and go that tract; but she opted more for the medical field. She had always wanted to be a Doctor and help make people feel better.

She had won a scholarship to attend college. Part of that scholarship money was for her to study medicine in an inner-city setting. Leslie had the goal to some day work at a major teaching hospital, where she could be sure to work her way through the ranks. She knew that her dedication and expertise in her field would get her far. Half way through her program, one of her colleagues was offered a position and gave up their scholarship. Leslie was asked to fill in their place "temporarily", until another candidate could be found. Reluctantly, she acquiesced, but soon found that she actually liked the job. When her tenure was up; she had made such a dramatic impact on her superiors that they asked her to stay on as lead doctor. She had made the conscious decision to stay where she was so that she could help many women who may not have otherwise never see a doctor.

All that was now being called into question if; somehow, Peter *did* trade into another ball club.

She knew that she would have to make some sort of decision as to what to do; but she told herself that she didn't have too much to worry about. Peter and his family was just going to have to accept the fact that Peter was not as great as they wanted him to be. Leslie knew; deep down in her heart, that she was going to have to be the primary breadwinner. Peter had a single-focus, and was not thinking logically. He was not; and had not, prepared himself for the time when his football career ended. Leslie was hoping for a miracle that somehow Peter would come to his senses.

As time went on; she grew more and more irritated with Peter and his parents. The more she spoke with them, the more convinced she was that he was not the right guy for her. She was looking for a way out; a way to get rid of Peter, with no way for him to ever want to reunite back with her. She could think of a thousand different illegal ways, but knew that she was not willing (or capable) of harming someone else.

She wanted to share this plight with her "sister-friends", but knew that this was something that she was just going to have to work out for herself. She was beginning to get to the end of her rope.

Then, there came some sort of light at the end of the tunnel. Peter got an invitation to open audition for a slot in an expansion team for the fledgling "Arena Football League". Peter was enthralled that he was getting another chance. Leslie; on the other hand, had to feign excitement. She knew that this was probably going to be the litmus test as to whether or not Peter was able to pass muster. She braced herself for the ultimate let-down that was sure to come.

Leslie was shocked when Peter called her from Vancouver, telling her that he actually had won a spot on the new team from Nova Scotia. Leslie's anxiety kicked into high gear. What was she going to do now? The one thing that she counted on was the fact that Peter was not ever going to get to play ball. Now; that he has a shot at making his dream come true, she didn't want any part of relocating. Now how was she going to get out of this?   She was for sure that Peter was going to try and pressure her into setting a wedding date so that he could get his life settled. Leslie knew that it was now "do-or-die" time. She had no other choice but to come clean with him about her feelings.

Peter couldn't wait to get home and celebrate his good fortune. He was now looking forward to now setting a wedding date.   He immediately contacted his parents to set the wheels in motion. He made one critical mistake; he failed to advise his potential bride that he had begun to make wedding plans without her input. He was soon to learn that this mistake was about to cost him his relationship forever. Not only did he make plans behind her back; but he swore his family to secrecy. Leslie had no idea that she was about to be blind-sided until it was too late.

Peter had a stroke of good luck. Bianca was

planning a holiday soirée; and Peter figured that it would be the most opportune time. He knew that all of Leslie's friends would be in attendance, so he wouldn't have to go out of his way to round everyone up. They'd all be there. He knew that he had about four months to get everything all together, and worked feverishly to proceed forward with his plans. Leslie was trying to set the stage to sit down and talk to him; but was thwarted at every turn. Peter suddenly was busier than he had ever been. Leslie was beginning to get more and more anxious; as his proposed training date crept closer and closer.

Chapter Seven

$\mathcal{T}$he girls had met one another within their first month of arriving to Ft. Lauderdale. Since the first day they met, they had become fast friends; alone they knew that they were just mere fishes swimming around in the same pond, together they posed a formidable school of piranhas; setting the standard by which all other women in their community are judged. Each of these women; in her own right, had attributes that commanded attention wherever they went. They played off of each other's similarities and differences to the hilt in order for the group to achieve its lofty (and rightful) place in society. As the years ticked by; however, a few cracks in the armor had begun to show. Not the usual, superficial cattiness, but serious melodrama began to unfold in each girls' life respectively and within the confines of the collective group.

Bianca and her husband of four months;
Caleb, decided to settle in Ft. Lauderdale
instead of Chicago when it was time for Caleb to
chose location he was going to chose to set up
his Law Firm. Caleb had studied with the best.
Fresh off of the O.J. Simpson trial, Caleb proved
invaluable as a key legal analyst and solid
documentarian. Johnnie Cochran himself helped
him secure the monies he needed to set up his
own practice. Caleb and Bianca knew that they
would fare much better in the warm climate of
Florida than up in the trenches of Chicago. For
any Black attorney, the south was a much better
option than up north; there was already a glut of
everything. Most professions have saturated the
market in such cities as Los Angeles, Chicago,
New York, DC and Atlanta.

The Ft. Lauderdale/Miami corridor still
remained sewn up by Jewish flight from up north.
Caleb wanted to get in and get a toe hold before
his chances were all but dried up. Bianca could

find a job anywhere. She had studied banking and finance, so she could market her skills in any number of fields. She settled on a small emerging company that was growing by leaps and bounds every quarter. Bianca's position as Vice President in charge of Acquisitions at Blockbuster's World Headquarters, located in Ft. Lauderdale kept her pretty busy. Every week she was jetting across the country scouting new for locations to open stores. She had become astute in acquiring failing Mom-and-Pop video stores; expanding their floor space and turning them into cash cows.

By the time her first year anniversary rolled around at both her job and in her marriage; Bianca was poised to make well over a million dollars in salary and stock options. She and Caleb were living the life they both had only dreamed of. They rented a small condo and squirreled their money away. For their anniversary; instead of splurging on a trip or a party for themselves, they put a hefty down payment on the construction of their new home in Parkland. It was during this time when they happened to all meet in the offices of Thrower, Betancourt and Stein; a full-service mortgage company that handled upscale clients. It was Michael Thrower that all of the girls had been referred to. Michael was the only black at this prestigious firm. These three young, brash men were courted by every socialite and wannabe socialite from Miami to West Palm Beach. Not only were these three impeccably groomed, but each had a physique, charm and personality about them that made them hugely marketable when it came to the ladies.

Gregoire "Greg" Betancourt was the "Dreamboat". His Greek/Portuguese ancestry gave him an ethnic look that was drop-dead gorgeous. His huge, expressive blue sapphire eyes twinkled whenever he laughed. And his long dark eyelashes made women go crazy. He had the dark, swarthy appeal of a Clark Cable mixed in with Antonio Banderas. His thick

Mediterranean accent made him even sexier to the ladies; along with some of the gentlemen clientele, too. Michael brought an air of forbidden lust. Michael had a look about him that harkened back to the Master-Slave times deep in the south. His full lips and highly accentuated cheekbones led one to believe he was West Indian; Jamaican or Bahamian. No one ever gave away his secret that he was "good ol' Cephus Barnes" from up there in Lake Worth, Florida. Just a stone's throw off of I-95 in West Palm Beach; with a little bit of creative plastic surgery, he was able to erase his old persona and create a totally new one. Just like his mentor and good friend from college, Herrman Nathaniel Weinstein had. Now; Nathaniel had big dreams to make his mark in the world. He wanted to be more than just the inheritor of his father's Kosher Delicatessen over in Sunrise Lakes. He needed to show to the world that he was able to make a difference in the world; if not, his own world. Nate, as he had preferred to be called, studied up at NYU, where the rest of his clan could look after him and keep an ever watchful eye on him, for his father's sake.

Upon graduation, Nathaniel was to come down and help run the family business. Nate had other plans. He never had any intention on taking over his father's store. His sister, Ida, was in much better position to do that, she was already doing everything that Nate should have been doing. He only thought it fair that her desperate whines go unheard. He would not tell her that he was never going to work at the store, he would show her. He shocked his family on the night of his graduation. He proclaimed that he was not going to return to Florida; he was going to set up shop in New York as a real estate agent. His family had thought that they were paying money for him to get a degree in business and accounting, but Nate had gotten his degree in accounting and real estate management. He managed to sock away all of the tips he had gotten over the years he was up there working through till his Master's;

and bought a small apartment complex that had been on Sheriff's sale. He was going into business with his college buddy, the new Michael Thrower, and they were going to rehab it and flip it for profit. His family was mortified, but within five years; they had managed to make a killing off of unwanted property throughout New York, and were now ready to set their sights on the crown jewel; Ft. Lauderdale.

During the plane ride down; at the lay over in Atlanta, the transformation of Cephus and Nate took place. They submitted their paper work to their respective state capitals and changed their names legally. They took many trips to South America to get plastic surgery to remove any vestiges of their former selves and to create the personas they were to become. Whereby Michael only needed to have his wisdom teeth removed to sink his cheeks in and plump them up with a few implants, Nate; now known as Ethan Stein, needed much more surgery to give him a more "Goy-ish" look. It took several nose jobs for him to be satisfied with the way it looked; and he even went as far as to have his "man-jewels" tweaked a bit to give it more girth. They couldn't make it longer, but they definitely could make it wider. He was finally satisfied when his Johnson was as thick as a polish sausage. Coupled with the fact that both he and Michael were working out in the gym every night; he felt that he would now able to get any woman he wanted. He didn't take into account that in Ft. Lauderdale, his appearance would also attract men. He had a strange dilemma on his hands. He decided to play it cagey. He would entertain the double-entendres from the guys, but would beg off of any propositions for late night sailings or weekend outings. Greg; on the other hand, saw it as a way to increase business sales. To him, it was all a part of his job. He wined and dined the customer; male or female, and let them sample his wares. He was by far, the top-producer of the three of them. Michael and Ethan didn't have it in them for *that* sort of customer satisfaction.

For Michael; having all five of the Divas sitting there in the lobby, waiting for him was a fantasy dream come true. He had not one, but five potential big moneyed clients that wanted him to show them properties. The only one who actually had an appointment was Bianca. The rest of them were just walk-ins. Michael decided to take a different approach with these ladies than he usually did his clients; and treated them as a "package deal". He brought them all into the conference room and made his presentation as if they were part of a special "promotion" that he had going on. He took full advantage of the audio-video capability that the room had and gave them all virtual tours based on the type of house each of them had in mind. Of the five; Allison was the one who seemed the most uninterested and unimpressed. She was; however, impressed with his partner; Ethan Stein. What captured her attention most was the fact that he seemed to have a little bit more going on down stairs than most of the other white men she's ever dated.

During a brief intermission, Allison begged off and told Michael's secretary that she decided that she was not interested in a "cattle call" to sell her a house. She wanted to speak to a manager about the way she was being treated. Ethan was summoned to the front desk and soon she was whisked away into Ethan's private office. When all was said and done; Allison not only had herself a home in the Rio Vista Development; she had the *only* home coveted by everyone in the Rio Vista Development and a brand new husband to boot! She and Ethan were married less than six months after they met. They weren't made for each other; but the sparks flew between the two of them whenever they got together. They had an odd kind of marriage, they truly weren't happy with one another unless they were arguing about something. Their most passionate lovemaking would come after some heated battles. It was usually over the most inconsequential things-more often than not over the nonchalant way she spent *his* money. He was no Donald Trump-yet; but she was spending money at the most exclusive shops as if he was. She would go into a store; go on a shopping spree buying whatever hit her fancy, and have the clerks charge it to her tab. Ethan would get the bill; hit the roof and then the sparks would fly. Ethan; on the other hand, looked forward to her antics. He wanted a wife; but knew he would not be satisfied with any of the Jewish-American Princesses that he knew wanted him. He wanted a woman that had some fire and passion "under the hood"; and had been told that either Black or Hispanic women were like Tigresses in bed. Allison proved this theory right, in his eyes. She was a challenge; not just some woman who would lay there and be non responsive. Allison would attack him; clawing at his back while they made love, flipping him around into different positions and trying every different kind of sex act his mind could dream up.

The rest of the girls did quite alright at Ethan's agency also. Michael worked diligently; coddling their projects through until he got them exactly what they wanted in an acceptable price range that they all were comfortable with. Bianca was the hardest one of the four. She and Caleb needed a "Showplace"; someplace spectacular that they would be able to entertain guests in; yet not have it feel like a museum. With the other three well on their way to their closings three months after they first stepped foot into the office, Michael felt a bit confident that he could guarantee Bianca that he could get the job done for her. His jaw dropped the morning she came into his office and plopped down the fact sheet in front of him. The place was a dump! "I know; I don't want it for the house, I want the land."

Michael worked with her night and day to get her the best people for the lowest possible cost. Bianca knew exactly what she wanted; she had researched all of the stores and knew the item names, numbers and UPC codes. All Michael had to do was follow her project guide book; it was all right there in print for him.

Chapter Eight

Reverend Willie Ray Thurston had a

commanding presence on the pulpit; as he
'peppered' his sermons with bodacious
interjections from the jazz band and choir. He
had been junior pastor ever since he stepped
foot in Ebenezer-Mount Zion United Brethren
A.M.E. Church. Prior to his coming there, there
were two churches: Ebenezer Zion and Mount
Zion A.M. E., both had failing attendance and
both were at war with each other. The Senior
Pastors from both churches had accused each
other for years of stealing congregants from each
other, and sabotaging each others edifices
whenever something bad had happened to either
one of them. Neither one was willing to concede
that they just could have just been vandalized by
some of the more "unseemly characters" as the
mothers of the church called them. Reverend
Willie Ray had no intention of ever stepping foot
in either one of these churches, he already knew

the reputations they had and the neighborhood they were situated in. Both of them were juxtaposed from one another right smack dab in the middle of a war zone.

The Sistrunk area of Ft. Lauderdale had been a hot bed of unrest for the past decade. In its heyday; it had been a community for Ft. Lauderdale's lower-to middle class Blacks. Now; it is a desolate jungle; full of drug dealers, prostitutes and derelicts. No; Willie Ray wanted no parts of this community or any of its congregates. As fate would have it, he happened to be in attendance the very same Sunday that they arrived.

The Right Bishop Cecil J. Paulson III had decided to grace his meager congregation and pontificate. It had been an unusually hot November Sunday; every sister sitting in the pews had been fanning themselves so hard that it sounded like a swarm of hummingbirds. The choir (if you could call it that) was comprised of the same core members it has always been since the beginning of time; so it seemed. Of course; Mother Paulson was the lead singer and choir mistress. All of the Paulson clan; in-laws included, had been corralled into singing. Which was a right mess; seeing as half of them couldn't carry a tune; even if you put it in a bucket for them. But; Bishop said, they posed a united front; a "bastion of decency in the midst of these troubled times." Bishop Paulson was often at odds with the majority of his congregation. He sequestered himself in his church and hardly ever ventured out into the community. He and his family didn't even live in Ft. Lauderdale proper anymore; they fled to the toney all-white suburbs of Parkland years ago.

   "And Jesus said; I cast ye out…in the name of all that is right and holy! By my father's command, I…" and when he drew in his breath, he had to swallow…hard. The doors to the chapel opened and four visions of loveliness stepped in; each one just as exquisite as the next. Not only did the Bishop's eyes nearly pop out of his head; but so did everyone else's who had turned around to catch a glimpse of these interlopers who had dared to interrupt the sermon. You could hear a collective gasp as everyone gave the four goddesses the once-over. There was more expensive millinery, baubles and accessories, which invariably made all of the mavens gawk and chatter about.

"Do you think that's a *real* Louis Vuitton bag she's carrying?" Hissed one of the old biddies.

"Did you see the rock on her finger? She must be dating one of those…what does my grandbaby call them…'ballers?" Whispered another.

"Girl; those *have* to be the same Jimmy Choo shoes I saw last week on "Sex and the City"; you know how much they cost? For all we know; they're probably 'professional women'…" Interjected yet still another old 'crone' to the other two.

All of the catty sniping and hushed whispering continued throughout the rest of the sermon. Leslie, Bianca, Brenda and remained cool and collected; taking it all in stride. Bianca knew that there was going to be a defining moment when they would unleash their 'Divadom' on them, and they will have the last laugh. It all came in the blink of an eye. More like the bat of an eyelash. Leslie's to be exact. She happened to be sitting in the pew across from Reverend Willie Ray and had was *not* amused by all that was going on around her, as were her friends. She was purveying her surroundings, critiquing the decorations and taking mental notes to report back once the girls were back in their own turf. During one of these perusals, she felt the stare of Reverend Willie Ray on her, and politely winked at him as she gave him a smile. His broad smile told her that something was on his mind. She pursed her lips at him and shook her head; as to advise him to get whatever unholy thoughts he was having about her out of his mind. She was only being cordial towards him; not inviting him to pursue her any further. Needless to say; that was not what Reverend Willie Ray interpreted in her wink.

Sister Ida Mae Jeter was having trouble finding the notes on the organ; constantly throwing the choir off-key. She had made it known that the piano was her forte'; so everyone forgave the hops and sliding keys she frequently found herself playing in. Bishop Paulson didn't make matters any better by trying to yell over the mistakes; he only made Sister Ida Mae play even louder; and more off key. The girls collectively looked at each other with the same countenance of disgust and disdain. One after another got up and exited the pew. Once again; the gasps rang out over the din; which angered Bishop Paulson. One by one; each girl marched up towards the pulpit and stood outward; facing the congregation, each girl striking her best and most church-appropriate 'Dreamgirls' pose. Bishop Paulson was not having this! "***And just what do you ladies think you're doing? This is MY church; this is MY choir, this is MY congregation! I am asking you to leave*** *quietly; as you can see the ushers are here to escort you out!"* He was motioning wildly; bobbing his head at his key henchmen for them to come and handle this situation.

The chaos that had ensued came to an abrupt halt with one silky sweet, syrup-y in tune; harmonized note from the girls. They sang "Amazing Grace" with such fluidity; poise, intonation, pitch and clarity that people began to close their eyes and become enraptured in their vocalizations. Everyone in that church was hypnotized by that one glorious sound. Each girls' voice meshed and blended in with one another; as if they were making love vocally. It was hard to tell where one voice began the stanza and when the other one ended it. There was not a flawed; sour or overpowering note to that hymn. By the end of the hymn; more tissues had been passed up and down the aisles than had ever been at *ANY* funeral this congregation had ever seen. Bishop Paulson was still standing there; his mouth gaping open; drool falling onto the pages of his sermon, his fingers were now digging holes into his skin from still being clenched in the fist he was using to punctuate his speech. He had been mystified. This was what he had been praying for all of his adult life; a choir that could move him to tears by just the sound of their voices. That had only happened to him once in his life. When he had received his calling; he had been listening to Mahalia Jackson at one of the revivals in his hometown of Biloxi, Mississippi. He'd searched and searched his whole lifetime to hear that magnanimous sound again. He had all but given up hope of ever finding it again, but here it was, standing right there in front of him. God had touched him and given him a sign that it was time; time for him to move on; time for him to let go and let someone else carry on with his work at this church. The feuding had now come to an end. He knew what he had to do. It was his time to retire. He uttered not another sound the rest of the service. He let the Deacons and Deaconesses complete the

service in his stead. He came down out of the
pulpit and sat with them in the front pew; his
head in his hands as he himself sobbed
uncontrollably. This was his final redemption.
"You ladies look like you could use a drink", Rev.
Willie Ray said, as he maneuvered himself
through the throngs of people and approached
the women; gently placing his fingertips on the
elbow of Allison as he ushered them towards the
refreshment table.
"Why, thank you…" Allison cooed as Rev. Willie
Ray positioned himself in between all of the
ladies and escorted them to their chairs once he
filled their demitasses full of lemonade.
"Why; it t'ain't no trouble a'tall, pretty lady"; he
crooned, with his smoothest Southern charm.

   For the rest of the afternoon, Rev. Willie Ray
commandeered the women's attention and
regaled in their stories of all of their other church
visits. He was eager to pick their brains and find
out what type of church these fine specimens of
womanhood would attend. His diligence didn't

go unnoticed. Bishop Paulson sent his henchmen around to get the buzz on what was happening. By the time the five ladies left; the whole congregation had queried them as to who they were, what they were doing there, if they were spying for another congregation, and if they were remaining as members. They wanted to have bragging rights as to the church that had sisters like them as congregants. This would ensure that their coffers (and pews) would be filled each and every Sunday with eager wealthy young Black men who would give his eye tooth to court one of the seemingly eligible bachelorettes. Of course; they would have to wait to see which one would end up being the wife of Rev. Willie Ray. If he decided to remain at that church himself. Bishop Paulson would have it no other way...

Chapter Nine

Bishop Paulson arranged a meeting with

Rev. Willie Ray immediately. He knew instinctively what needed to be done; that it was time for the changing of the guard, the writing was on the wall.

"You know; son, many a young minister's had their eye on my chuch…"

"Yessir; I know".

"Are you one of them?"

"Yessir; I believe I am."

"And what makes you think stand out head and shoulders above the other candidates; may I ask?"

"Well; suh…I come highly regarded by all of the other Senior Pastors I have stood in for."

"You know; the one thing that makes you un-marketable…in my book that is?"

"Naw, suh…"

"You are a bachelor. A single Reverend in a

congregation is about as bad as inviting a rooster into the hen house after dark."

He knew that the Bishop was right. Nothing divided congregations quicker than a single Reverend. It was too much of a distraction. Willie Ray had to think of something quick to say before his chances died.

"Well; suh…" I may be single now; but I do have a fiancée waiting for me back home in Detroit."

"Well, son, when is the big day planned?"

"She wanted to wait until I found a permanent church. Her folks didn't want me on the road as much as I am. They wanted me to settle down in one city before they would allow her to entertain the thought of ever marrying me. You know she was here today…?"

"Don't tell me that one of those fine young sisters that were here today was…?"

'Yessir…one of those was the future Mrs. Reverend Dr. Willie Ray Thurston."

Willie Ray knew that he was playing with dynamite the moment he formulated the thoughts in his brain, but he was bound and determined to make one of those five women his bride. His whole career depended on it. As he handed Bishop Paulson his credentials; he added:

"A feather in the cap of this church will be having my fiancée and her friends singing up in the choir every Sunday." He was really reaching for it, and he knew it. He was placing his bets that once he made one of those ladies his wife, she would be able to persuade her friends to perform at least a few songs per year to keep the congregation (and Bishop) happy.

Bishop Paulson went over his credentials with a fine-tooth comb. He queried him on the most minute detail. Finally; after an hour and a half, he concluded his interview.

"I'm not going to promise you anything; I still have a short list of other candidates I am interviewing."

Willie Ray knew that the Bishop was bullshitting him. This church was strapped for cash and needed a jolt to get the congregation jump-started again. Willie Ray knew that with one of the 'Divas' behind him, he would be able to make that church rival any of the other now-famous churches in the country. His name would be synonymous with the likes of Rev. C.L. Franklin, Bishop T. D. Jakes, Rev. D. J. Kennedy and The Rev. Billy Graham.

Chapter Ten

*T*he time had come and Charmaine knew it;
she had to return home and face the truth. She
could not go on another day; she had to confront
her father, some how make him confess his sins
to his congregation and pay retribution to her and
her mother for what he had done to the family.
She would have it no other way; she no longer
would let this memory rule her life; prohibit her
from going forward and falling in love. She did;
however, have to decide whether or not she was
going to tell "the girls". She knew deep down in
her heart that they would stand by her side in
whatever decision she would ultimately make;
but for some reason, she wanted to keep this
part of her life all to herself. Yes, it was best that
she did it first and then told them the whole story
once she came back…*if* she ever came back.

As Charmaine packed her suitcase for the
trip back home; she had to make a major

decision; just how was she going to confront her father? She knew that she would be risking everything by doing this, so she scrapped her plans to fly home, it was too short of a trip and she needed more time to formulate a plan. So she decided to take the train. It would give her a day and a half, with all of the stops to sort through all of the pros and cons before she got there. Charmaine told the girls that her mother had summoned her back home because her father had suddenly taken ill, so that easily explained her abrupt departure, and promised to call every night to update them on his progress. She hated lying to her friends but knew that they would forgive her once they knew the reason she had to.

As the train finally pulled into the station in Little Rock, Charmaine's adrenaline began to surge. She had her plan in place, and was ready to carry it out. She decided not to stay at her parent's house; it was just too creepy, too many bad memories. And besides; she wouldn't have the leverage she needed by being up underneath them. No; she needed distance away from them so that they wouldn't feel betrayed by her sleeping under their roof and then dropping an atomic bomb in their lap.

"Momma; it's me, Charmaine, just calling to let you know that I'm back home for a few days."

"Well, baby, you could have stayed here in your own house."

"I know; I just wanted to be able to come and go as I pleased. I didn't want to be a burden on you and Daddy in the event I stayed out late with some of my old girlfriends."

"Now, you know that's just not true…you wouldn't be a burden. You and your sister…"

"I know, Momma, this is our house and we are always welcomed there at any time."

"That's right; you're just talking nonsense…a burden to me and your father…"

"Momma…can we have some '*us*' time together; soon?"

"What do you mean by 'us' time; baby is

everything ok?"

"Yeah; I am just missing having long quiet talks with my Momma, that's all."

"Well, now; let me see…I got ladies auxiliary meeting on Tuesday; Choir rehearsal on Wednesday,
bible study Thursday…"

"Anything tomorrow?"

"Monday nights I volunteer at the Senior Center."

"Well; how about setting some free time for me next week?"

"Yeah; that would be best. I could plan for it a bit better."

"So; I'll stop by in the morning and we'll plan a date for next week, Ok?"

"Ok…see you tomorrow baby."

"Love ya, Momma."

"And I love you too, baby."

Charmaine felt as if the weight was starting to move from on top of her heart as she hung up.

Chapter Eleven

*A*llison knew that Brenda was not being told
the truth by Chad. Things just weren't adding up;
and Brenda wasn't noticing what was right in
front of her. They had all known that something
just wasn't jiving with Chad's story about his past;
so Allison decided to get to the bottom of it and
get to the truth. The very first thing that she did
was contact her friend "in the business", Valerie
to see what she knew about him; or what dirt she
could dig up on him.

"Girl; I hope you don't have plans to marry that
man." Valerie told her; off-handedly.

"Why... should I be concerned?"

"Girl; you know that you're one of my best "friend-
girls" in the whole wide world, so you know that I
wouldn't do or say anything intentionally to hurt
you...right"

Allison's heart was beginning to race; she was
about to get the "4-1-1" she had wanted. She

knew that she had to play it cagey.

"Yeah; I know. I just get the feeling that he's not telling me the whole truth…y'know?"

"Baby…the truth is that he's playing for both teams."

"Really?" Allison feigned naiveté. She knew she was right!

"Chile'…your man has been linked to several different high-profile brotha's that are on the `DL'.

"DL?" Allison poured it on…but good! She knew exactly what the DL meant. She had been "of the world", and knew what was going on. She just wanted Valerie to "spill her guts" as much as possible so that Allison had enough evidence to present to Brenda. After several hours of chatting with her friend; in which she had pumped her full of lies about how she had suspected Chad of cheating, and the pictures of him with all of the gay icons, and the fact that she had never heard of "Falcon Club" models. This was not entirely true. She just couldn't remember *how* she knew about them. When Valerie told her; she instantly wanted to puke. She remembered that she had seen a few of the "Falcon Club" videos at one of her gay friend's house. Suddenly, everything became crystal clear…Chad was; at one time, a porn star! She wanted to call up Brenda and tell her all about her "man"; but knew that it could only blow up in her face. She had to come up with a way to tell her so that she would be believed. But how? She needed a plan…

Allison seemed to be in a bit of a quandary herself. She and Rev. Willie Ray had started seeing each other, and for the Reverend, it was getting pretty serious. He had a deadline to meet, and goods to deliver. Allison wasn't all that sure whether or not she could now date a man of the cloth. Not that she didn't like Rev. Willie Ray; she just didn't see herself as a "Minister's wife." She wasn't so sure that this was what she wanted for herself, but the Rev. Willie Ray was persistent. He was not going to give up on trying to win Allison's hand'; and possibly effect the biggest coup in church history. There was just no way that he was going to let Allison slip out of his fingers; have his dreams go up in smoke.

Chapter Twelve

*T*he time had come for Charmaine to return home. She had seen enough of her stepfather's ugliness to last her the rest of her life, and no matter how many times she tried to intervene on her mother's behalf; but each time her mother took the side of her husband. Charmaine had enough; she knew that she was fighting a losing battle; that her mother was not going to leave him, no matter what anyone said. She was "old school"; she had been raised with the notion that she was useless without a man. She was not one of those "newfangled" women who had been emancipated during the sixties. Charmaine knew that Gladys Ann Simiwell was going to stay married to Lemuel Simiwell until the day she died; which could come sooner than she thought if Lemuel kept beating on her. The air had been thick with contention between the three of them; Lemuel lording his authority; showing off in front of Charmaine by forcing Gladys to be at his beck and call. The more Lemuel strutted; the more Charmaine challenged his authority.

It all came to a head the Saturday evening before they all went to bed. Charmaine had spent her days visiting relatives and friends; just hanging out around town. She was just a few blocks away from the family home, when one of her young cousins came tearing through the house, out onto the back porch, where she and her cousin Irma had been getting re-acquainted over cold glasses of sweet tea. "'Scuze me; cousin Charmaine…" the faint voice panted; her face flushed from apparently running at break-neck speed. Charmaine sensed that something terrible was happening; for without any sound; she leaped up from the rocking chair and bolted down the steps, Irma frantically trying to keep up. "Girl; you don't want to get involved; they go through this all the time. Sheriff Biggsley just stopped coming at all to see what was the matter. He got tired of wasting his time over a false alarm". Charmaine stopped dead in her tracks so suddenly that Irma ran smack into her and fell over backwards.

"What the hell do you mean? Am I hearing you correctly that Sheriff Biggsley *refuses* to come by and see what is going on?"

Irma was trying to catch her balance; regain her footing so that she could answer Charmaine. Charmaine just stood over her; her hands on her hips, looking as if she wanted to fight someone. "Well?... I'm waiting for an answer..."

Irma knew that she had to think quick, for she knew that Charmaine was not going to stand by and let her mother be beaten on and no one come to her rescue. Irma knew that there was going to be hell to pay; she just didn't want to be the one to pay for it also.

"I call every time they get into a rau; but Sheriff Biggsley just tells me to mind my own business."

Charmaine raised her head, squared her shoulders and closed her eyes to a slit. Irma could tell by her silence that Charmaine was about to get to business! Charmaine opened her mouth; but Irma had to strain to hear what she was saying. Charmaine spoke softly; with a serene calmness that told Irma instinctively to walk away; gather her kids and remain in the house until she given a sign that it was "all clear".

She wasn't exactly sure what that sign would be, or where who it would be coming from; but nonetheless, she knew that she had to wait it out. No matter how long it took.

As Irma picked up her gait; she constantly would look back to see if Charmaine had left, and finally realized that she was waiting for her to gather her children and ensconce them in the house.

Irma had done what she was told; and after feeding and bathing all of her children, she put them to bed early. This was the one time that she had broken her own rule of not allowing the children sleep with her. She allowed them to tell stories and play amongst themselves; *anything* to keep them close by.

When Charmaine knew that Irma was safely

behind closed doors, she steeled herself for the task at hand. It was a showdown; and she was ready. It was a long time coming, and she figured Lemuel had it coming to him. Charmaine could hear the screams of her mother and the crashing of furniture as Lemuel batted her around. The odd thing; to her, was that the neighbors were all behaving as if nothing was happening. Charmaine's blood began to boil. How could they just sit by and let a defenseless woman get beaten? She wondered. Then she got a big slap of reality. Each and every woman that she saw had the same look on their faces; that look of shame and disgrace. For each of them had been privy to one another's beatings. Not one of them had been spared. It was part of an every day occurrence.

Charmaine's walk back to her parent's house was slow and deliberate. She wanted to catch her stepfather off guard; and knew that if the neighbors saw her rushing towards the house, they might tip him off. She then decided not to come in through the normal way; straight down Center Square Road, she took the back dirt roads that circumvented the main thoroughfare. This way; she felt certain that she would be able to be undetected. The closer she got to home, she could hear the racket that was going on inside. Form where she was positioned, she knew that coming in through the back door would surely be a waste of time. He would have ample time to bolt out the door and get away. Charmaine had to think and act quickly. It came to her in a split second. She remembered how she used to sneak out and back into the house whenever she was on punishment; and decided that it was her best element of surprise.

She shimmied up the oak tree that she used so effectively before. Since she always left her bedroom window open so that she could blow the smoke out it; so as not to contaminate the rest of the house, she easily climbed back in through it. She utilized the stealth tactics she had employed so as not to be detected in the past, as she made her way down the stairs to place herself in a more advantageous position to pounce at a moments notice. She arrived at the precise time her mother needed her most.

"I told you I didn't want that harlot here in my house; didn't I?" He said as he backhanded his wife across the face; with such a force that she lost her balance and crashed into a curio cabinet. Lemuel took several steps towards his wife, but was stopped instantly in his tracks as he felt the sting of a knife graze past his right shoulder. Lemuel spun around and came face to face with his Charmaine.

"Who the hell do you think you are; coming into my house and threatnin' me with a knife. Bitch; I'll kill you!" He shouted at her.

"Not if I kill you first!" Charmaine snorted; her blood was coursing hot through her veins at the chance of settling the score between she and her father. She knew that one of them was not going to make it out of this unscathed. Before Lemuel could draw in his next breath, Charmaine had

hurled another dagger at him which hit its mark.
He immediately clutched his right shoulder and
ripped the dagger from where it had landed.
Charmaine had already started approaching her
mother; never taking her icy stare off him. The
look in her eyes told Lemuel that she meant
business. In a desperate attempt to scare
Charmaine off; Lemuel lobbed the dagger at his
wife. He knew that Charmaine would do anything
in her power to protect her mother; who now lay
in a heap, semi-conscious.

Lemuel didn't know what Charmaine knew. She
knew that his toss was weak and ineffective. The
dagger wobbled about for a couple of feet and
landed with a weak "plop" a few inches away
from Gladys' feet.

   Lemuel instantly feared for his life. He had no
other defense but to fight Charmaine hand-to-
hand, and one of his fighting arms was rendered
incapacitated by the dagger. Charmaine began to
pull her mother to safety. Lemuel thought to
himself that this was his only chance, so he

lunged out and grabbed hold of Gladys' ankles; ripping her right out from Charmaine's grasp.

"She ain't goin' nowhere wit' you; so get outta my house. We don't want your ass here no more!" He spat.

"When I leave; I'm taking my mother with me!". She snapped back at him.

"Over my dead body!" Lemuel retorted. A sinister look washed over Charmaine.

"As you wish…" Charmaine said; with a deadpan iciness and determination. Lemuel became enraged; but felt powerless. He knew that now he was no match for Charmaine. He needed a distraction. But what? Just then, there was a knock on the door.

"Mr. Sidiwell; this is the sheriff. Open up!" Lemuel's face lit up like a child's on Christmas morning.

"We'll see who leaves this house now; bitch!" He hissed. As Lemuel flung open the door; he put on his best theatrical performance.

"She's trying to kill me!" He wailed; as he rushed

out onto the porch, dripping in blood.

"Calm down, Mr. Simiwell. It's only a flesh wound. By this time; the neighbors had started gathering around to see first-hand the spectacle that was unfolding.

Charmaine had been devoting her time to tending to her mother; getting her revived and back on her feet. Sheriff Holloway was trying to corral everyone back to their own domiciles.

"Go on; now, nothing here to see. Not like you guys haven't had your own share of problems." When it didn't seem as if the crowd was going to disperse, Sheriff Holloway started shoo'ing them all away.

"Go on; now, git!"

One by one the crowd started heading back to their own houses, and Sheriff Holloway was able to re-focus on the Sidiwells.

"Now; what happened here?"

Lemuel told Sheriff Holloway that he and his wife had been having a "little husband and wife thing"; and stated that Charmaine overreacted and came at him with a knife.

"That's odd;" Sheriff Holloway replied. "Your neighbors tell me that they heard your wife screaming and the breaking of furniture long before Charmaine came on the scene. They say that the only voices they initially heard were just you and your wife's. How do you explain that?"

Lemuel stood silent; for he knew what was going to come out of the Sheriff's mouth, he had been warned once before and was told what was going to happen the next time they were involved in one of their now famous "arguments".

"But…She stabbed me with a knife; huh, what about that? Is she just going to get away with attempted murder?"

Lemuel knew it; as soon as the words fell from his lips, that Sheriff Holloway was going to challenge him on his last statement.

"And how do you explain all of this?" Sheriff Holloway asked; with raised eyebrow. The house was in shambles. There was no denying that something more than just an argument had taken place.

"I...I...can explain." Lemuel started. Sheriff
Holloway waved at him.

"No need. I wouldn't believe you anyway."
Lemuel felt defeated. He knew that he was now
rendered powerless in front of both his wife and
the daughter that he detested.

As Sheriff Holloway stepped inside and took a
statement from both Gladys and Charmaine;
Lemuel had been instructed to remain on the
porch, a mere by-stander. After assessing the
situation inside the home; Sheriff Holloway
stormed out on the porch and summarily
handcuffed Lemuel, charging him with assault
and battery on his wife. Lemuel felt humiliated as
he was escorted to the cruiser and was taken
away.

Charmaine stayed behind and tended to her
mother; trying to illicit any kind of response from
her as to what set Lemuel off this time.

"Child; you know how he is..." her mother said.

"Yes; and I'm also aware of the fact that he can

potentially kill you." Charmaine warned; her
mother seemed oblivious to that fact.

"Oh; stop being so melodramatic. Lemuel loves
me. You're just jealous; you've always been,
even as a little girl. You never wanted me to be
happy. You never wanted me to marry him."

"Do you know why?" Charmaine asked.

"Why what?" Gladys asked; rather agitated.

"Why you don't like my choice of husband; is *that*
what you mean?"

Charmaine really wanted to spare her mother the
truth about Lemuel; but her anger got the best of
her. It had to come out at some point; she just
thought that it would have been at a more
advantageous time.

"Mama; he repeatedly raped me."

"Child; stop spreading those filthy lies on him!"
Her mother retorted. Still; Charmaine insisted.
She had to; in order for her mother to open her
eyes and face the truth.

"Why do you think I always wanted to tag along
with you every time you left the house? He would

rape me every time we were alone together."
Charmaine's eyes welled up with tears from
holding onto this secret all of these years. Her
voice was low; calm and steady. When she
spoke; she hung her head in shame.

"I lost several of his bad…"

"*NO!* Don't you dare tell that lie on him!" Gladys
screamed. "I now see that he was right; you *have*
been trying to break us up ever since he came
into my life."

Charmaine could feel her heart breaking with
each and every word; her own mother choosing a
stranger over her own flesh and blood.

Charmaine's tears were flowing like a river. She
now knew what she had to do. She must do the
unthinkable to get her mother to pay attention to
her. The last words she heard her mother say to
her as she climbed the stairs to her room to pack
was;

"Lemuel loves me; you never gave him a chance.
I know I haven't been a perfect wife to him; he's a
good man. You just want me to end up like

you…alone and unloved." Her mother's words trailing up the stairs; piercing straight through her spine into her heart.

Chapter Thirteen

When Charmaine had finished packing; she took out her cell phone and contacted "The Girls" to let them know that she was on her way home. She then gathered up her belongings and made her way downstairs. It was the last time that she would ever communicate with her; and probably the last time she would ever have her mother hear her words. Charmaine knew; deep in her heart, that her mother would be dead once she left. It would only be a matter of time before Lemuel went too far. As she passed by her mother's room, she could hear her muffled sobbing through the door. She towards the kitchen to leave for her mother a heart-felt letter and long-overdue package. She steeled herself as she continued to make her way down the steps. A few moments later the taxi was there; sounding its horn.

As she approached the doorway; her mother's

voice feeble voice called to her.

"Charmaine...you still here?" Charmaine let out a long and heavy sigh.

"Good-bye; Momma." She whispered; as she turned the knob.

"Baby; please...why didn't you tell me sooner. I am sooo sorry."

Charmaine's knees buckled as she heard her mother's unsteady footsteps on the stairs. As the taxi sped off; Gladys held her daughter in a motherly embrace, their sobs echoing through the dark, quiet, empty house.

"Why didn't you dispose of the fetuses years ago?" Gladys asked.

"I was afraid; ashamed. I didn't know what to do. I then decided that I would get even with the both of you and use them when the time was right. I knew that *someday* I would get you to listen to me"; Charmaine wailed. Gladys rubbed her daughter's back as she "shushed" her. When she finally got Charmaine to calm down some; she had her recount the ordeal that Lemuel had put her through. Gladys could never forgive herself for not being there for her daughter in her time of need. Now her daughter needed her the most; and she knew she had to be strong for her. No matter how much it hurt; she knew that her daughter had to have someone to tell her ordeal to. Not like Gladys; who had to burden her ordeal all by herself. Young, frightened, alone, emotional. She had to wake up everyday and face her molesters as if nothing happened. Not to mention the excruciating agony she endured as she aborted all of her own stepfather, uncles and brothers' offspring.

Gladys thought that she had suppressed those memories decades ago; that she was safe from the horrific nightmares she had endured as a young woman. They were staring her dead in her face now and she couldn't hide from them any longer. As she scooped up the box of decomposed, mummified fetuses, she knew just how to make the pain stop for the both of them. But first, she had to get her surviving daughter to sleep. As Charmaine drifted off to sleep with the warm milk concoction; she put her plan into action. Her midnight visit with both the Rev. Goins and Sheriff Holloway set a chain of events into motion that she could never have anticipated.

Charmaine called upon her "girls" to help her get through her ordeal. They were more than happy to drop everything and come rushing to her aid. They spent the whole day Saturday cleaning up her mother's house, and getting her packed and ready to relocate with Charmaine. All throughout the day, they listen intently as both Charmaine and Gladys divulged their shared secrets. It prompted each of the girls to come clean with their story of the men in their lives who had raped each and every last one of them. A few were fortunate enough not to have become pregnant. When tallied, there were 15 children aborted between the remaining four of them. Out of all of them; Charmaine was the sole survivor of Gladys' final rape before she was old enough to

flee her family homestead. Gladys had finally told
her daughter the truth about her birth. Gladys
had always told her that her father had died
during the Vietnam War. It was less complicated
than telling her that she wasn't sure if she was
the offspring of either her stepfather, one of her
four uncles or three brothers that raped her
constantly. Sometimes in succession; against her
will. They went through several boxes of tissues
as they cleaned; cried, laughed, hugged and
shared intimate moments.

   Sunday morning service came soon enough,
and the girls were ready. They had each purged
some major demons and were ready to go on
with their lives. Lemuel had been released from
jail, and was to stop by and pick up his
belongings before he was to get on a train back
to Mississippi to go and live with his family; as
the arrangement had been made. Reverend
Goins decided to change his sermon at the last
minute; in light of the information he had been
privy to. He decided to do something he had

only done several other times during his position as pastor. He was "ad-libbing it". He was speaking from his heart, speaking on-the-fly. As he closed his eyes and gave up his free will; the words spewed forth from him like a fountain of anointed elixir. Reverend Goins spoke words that touched every soul of his congregation. He didn't hold back; he chastised those who thought that they were above reproach; he lacerated those in his congregation who smiled up in his face, yet scandalized his name and robe once they step foot out of the church door.

He scoured the room and blasted those in his congregation who were hypocrites, adulterers, fornicators, liars, substance abusers, gossips, meddlers, substance abusers, gamblers, agitators and down-right malicious. He told them all that not one of them had the right to turn their nose up at anyone else; not even he or his wife. Reverend Goins turned the microscope on himself and told some of the dirt he had done in his life. He asked for his congregation's forgiveness, and told them that he pledged to uphold the same moral compass that he was now charging them. The congregation was re-charged and had broken into song when suddenly the parish doors flung open and in stormed Lemuel brandishing a pistol.

"Where is she?" He snorted.

"My brother…there's no need for violence. God…."

"Aww; shut the hell up; Reverend!" Lemuel shouted, as he fired off a round in the church ceiling. Congregants cowered in the pews as Lemuel started making his way down the aisle; flailing the gun around haphazardly. Two thirds of the way down; he spotted Charmaine, his intended prey.

"Get up, you fuckin' bitch. We got some unfinished business to tend to!"

Charmaine stood up and made her way defiantly towards the center pew; much to the dismay of her friends, who were tugging at her clothing to get her to sit back down.

"I'm right here; pull the trigger. I have nothing to lose; I've made my peace with the Lord… have you?" She said calmly, as she stood in the center of the aisle. Lemuel had a clear shot of her; he could take it at any chance.

"Are you sure?" He asked as he pointed the gun directly at her. Charmaine closed her eyes and raised her head up to the sky; she was ready to meet her maker.

"Drop your weapon!" She heard someone shout.

'Fuck you; you dyke bitch! You don't scare me. Everyone knows that you're a woman underneath that uniform."

"I'm warning you; Lemuel Sidiwell. Put down that gun!" Sheriff Holloway repeated.

"Go to hell; bitch!" Lemuel spat.

Charmaine then heard two rapid-fire shots; one slightly louder than the other, and then pandemonium broke loose. When she opened her eyes; Lemuel lay dead where he stood; her mother was slumped over in her pew.

"***Momma!***" Charmaine screamed as she rushed

to her side.

"I'm…I'm alright; baby. Call me an ambulance, though." When Charmaine turned to ask for a cell phone to call an ambulance, she saw that she didn't need one. Sheriff Holloway was there; on the walkie-talkie already calling for one.

Gladys was carted off to the nearest hospital, and treated for a gunshot wound to her chest. She was lucky that she was sitting the way she was; as the bullet stopped fractions of an inch away from her heart. A few days later, Lemuel Sidiwell was laid to rest. Gladys had been kept company by all of the girls, helping to speed her recovery. Neither she nor Charmaine attended the funeral. Charmaine did; however, escort her to the grave site once she was released from the hospital to pay her last respects. Time flew by quickly and soon it was time for Charmaine and her friends to be heading back to their own lives. Gladys had been recovering well enough, and her therapy sessions were coming along better than the doctors had anticipated. The girls became an instant hit around the neighborhood; being invited to all of Charmaine's friends and relative's homes. Charmaine replayed the same scenario that started the whole fiasco, when she and her friends visited her cousin back on her porch for some sweet teas.

Bianca proposed a toast to all of them; for being there for their sister/friend in her time of need. As they all sipped on their drinks, Charmaine spoke up.

"I have been giving this a lot of thought; and have decided not to return to Ft. Lauderdale with you guys." There were several minutes of uneasy silence.

"My mother needs me; more than ever now that she is widowed. As you know; we have begun to talk to each other and patch up years of distance between us." She went on to say. Each girl knew, deep in their hearts, that she was doing the right thing. If any one of them were in her shoes; they'd do the same thing. They all hugged as they ended their final evening together. And they vowed to keep in touch and visit one another every chance they got, the next afternoon as they said their good-bye's at the airport. Charmaine handed over the key to her house to Bianca; who was to make all the arrangements to get it packed up and shipped to her. The rest of the girls were enlisted to exact other parts of their plan to get Charmaine ensconced into her new life back at home with her mother.

   Once Charmaine knew that her friends were safely on their way back home; she could concentrate her efforts on helping her mother. She knew what pressure Gladys faced each and every day, and knew that although her mother said she was fine; she knew that she had not yet started the long and painful process of grieving. Gladys still had to come to terms with the fact that her oppressor was finally dead. Her hell on earth was over. She didn't know how to live on her own; didn't know if she was fully capable of it. Her whole life had been in Lemuel. She had no other skill or training other than being a housewife and mother. Gladys didn't want to think about her life; the more Gladys thought about it, the more she saw how helpless she was. Lemuel had been right all along. She truly did need him to take care of her. She saw Charmaine as the woman she had always wanted to become but was afraid of; confident, sure of herself, independent, wealthy, opinionated, learned. All of the things that she wasn't. Charmaine soon began to settle into a role of domesticity; helping to care for her mother like she was. She surprised Gladys by showing her all of the skills she had taught her while growing up. Charmaine pampered her mother with good; down-home cooking. Gladys didn't believe it at first; not until Charmaine set her up in the parlor and went off into the kitchen. Gladys had feigned sleep, so that she could spy on her daughter; catch her in the act of passing off store-bought food as her own. Or even worse yet, passing off the neighbors' food as her own.

Gladys was sure she would bust her. Gladys was pleasantly surprised to find her daughter; elbow deep in flour, milk and eggs, beating and mixing up homemade cake batter. Gladys surveyed the room and saw all of her favorites at different stages of completion. A lump welled up in her throat, as she held back the tears. Her baby girl was throwin' down; taking *reeeeeeeal* good care of her Momma! Gladys felt a sense of pride and gratitude that Charmaine was able to put aside the past and allow both of them to come together and heal.

   Just as Gladys got herself situated back into her comfortable position on the couch; there came a knock at the door.

"Sit; Momma, I'll get the door!" Charmaine ordered.

Gladys sank herself back into her previous position. She kept ear one trained toward the foyer to catch the dialogue coming from that vicinity.

"Sheriff?..." Charmaine asked; semi-perplexed.

Gladys' heart began to race uncontrollably. Her peaceful respite had come to an end. She braced herself for what was surely to be next.

Sheriff Holloway tipped her hat and stood in the entranceway to the foyer.

"What brings you by this way; sheriff?" Gladys heard Charmaine ask.

"Just stopped by to pay my final respects; is all" she replied.

Gladys could hear nervous feet rustling about out there. She called out

"Well; as long as you're here, you might as well sit for dinner."

"Naw; Ma'am, don't mean to be impolite..."

"Well then don't be. Charmaine said, rather sternly.

"We could both use the comp'ny." Gladys chimed. From where she was sitting, she couldn't see the two of them staring at each other awkwardly. All she could hear was the faint; distant shuffling of feet. After a few moments of silence; Gladys raised herself up off of the couch to get a better look as to what was going on. She quickly plopped herself back down in her spot; stunned by what she had just witnessed.

Chapter Fourteen

Charmaine ushered Randi into the kitchen, where she felt that they would be safe enough to talk.

"So; why did you come here? You know how risky this can be for you." She said; just above a whisper.

"I know; but I'm ready to face the music. I've lived my life in hiding for far too long." Randi replied.

"I'm ready to walk away from this job; if need be. I need to have a life of my own for a change."

"Yeah, but..." Charmaine began, but Randi covered her mouth with her index finger.

"Let me worry about this; sweetheart. You have WAY too much on your plate right now to be dealing with my problems. Besides; I 'm a big girl, I can make decisions on my own." Randi flashed her a big smile.

Charmaine quieted down; and they just sat across the kitchen table from each other, holding each other's hands and staring at each other. Gladys' curiosity got the best of her when she noticed that she didn't hear the usual noises one would hear coming from the kitchen; so she got up off the couch and went to go and see what was happening for herself. She was a bit surprised to find them juxtaposed from one another; Charmaine bent over the kitchen counter, mindlessly nursing a cup of coffee; Randi leaning against the oven handle; staring blankly at the linoleum squares on the floor. Gladys slipped in; seemingly unnoticed, made herself something to eat, went and sat down at the kitchen table to "observe". Charmaine and Randi went about their lives as if they were in their own apartment. They interacted with each other cordially, both with an air of indifference towards each other. Gladys knew that there was something going on between the two of them that neither one was talking about. She just wasn't sure if she was ready to find out what.

"Randi?" Gladys chimed up.

"Ma'am?" Randi replied; in a monotone voice, that was barely audible.

'What seems to be botherin' you, honey?" When Randi didn't answer; she figured something must really have been wrong.

"Randi?" She asked again; this time with a bit more sense of urgency in her voice.

Randi raised her head; her eyes glazed over as if the dam was about to burst and let a torrent flood of tears.

"Baby; what's wrong?" Gladys asked; as she raised herself up from her chair and began to make her way towards Randi.

"Nothing; ma'am, I'm just tired…tired of all of this…" and she caught herself. She almost divulged her secret. The secret that she had sworn she would never tell.

By this time; Gladys had enveloped Randi into her bosom and began to rock her back and forth; as she had done her own children whenever they needed consoling. She began to hum one of the many gospel hymns that were in her repertoire.

They were low; soulful, old-time hymns, the ones that guaranteed you were going to need a box of tissues before they were over. Gladys had known how to bring out the pain, suffering and sorrow from the darkest recesses where it was hiding. She had spent many a years practicing; humming them to herself whenever she was getting a good ol' fashioned ass whoopin' from her husband. What she hadn't counted on was the fact that Randi was of a different background and upbringing than she. No matter which hymn she tried; Randi just would not give in and break down. Gladys finally gave up and hugged Randi as tightly as she could.

"It's gonna be alright; none of this was your fault." Gladys whispered; out loud. Not only to Randi, but as an affirmation to herself *and* to Charmaine. She felt God touch her heart and tell her that those words had to be said so that the healing process could begin. Randi collapsed into her arms like a rag doll; sobbing uncontrollably.

"There; there now, baby. It's alright." Gladys said softly, as she stroked Randi's silky, close cropped dark brown hair.

"My foster mother used to say that to me all the time." Randi uttered; just as softly.

Gladys was shocked to hear that Randi had been a foster child. She then surmised that to the outside public, she didn't look like a woman who had been a battered wife all her adult life, either. Her heart went out to Randi. Poor thing.

After several minutes of uncontrolled sobbing; Randi regained her composure and the three of them sat around the kitchen table; no one uttered a sound. All three of them staring blankly off into the distance. It was Randi who ultimately broke the silence by recounting the circumstances that brought her into foster care. Randi told of how her father was a mean drunk, who sexually abused she and her other sisters, but Randi more frequently than the others because she was younger and had a natural affinity for her father. Randi had placed her father on a pedestal. He had been her rock and hero after their mother abandoned the family to go off with a smooth talking musician that blew into town to play for one of the local gin joints on the outskirts of town. Randi idolized her father because he vowed to keep the family together in the face of adversity; when his own brothers and sisters agreed to take his children and raise them for him. Randi stated that she was conflicted with the feelings that she had of her father, for initially, she saw her father as a loving, warm, caring parent. Her sisters; however, constantly painted a different picture of him.

Randi had always considered her sisters as ungrateful to her father; who worked a full time job as a patrolman, and then worked any overtime to help fill in the gaps that his wife's paycheck used to cover. Randi knew that things had been a bit lax around the house; but she thought that her sisters abandoned the family too early. She soon learned; as she got older, the real reason why they had left. Her father began to sexually molest her; telling her that she reminded him so much of her mother. It got worse whenever he would get drunk. There were too many nights that Randi woke up to her father's drunken advances. Randi felt sorry for him; he lost his wife, then lost his children one by one. Randi promised him that she would never leave him; that she would do whatever he wanted her to, if he would just keep her safe. To Keenan Malrooney; his daughter Rhianna was his saving grace. She would accept him for who he was and didn't put up a fuss or refuse him whenever he made advances towards her. Keenan was able to do things with his daughter that his wife would balk at. He knew his daughter loved him unconditionally; and he was able to show her how much he loved her back-the only way he knew how.

Gladys sat there; stunned. She couldn't believe what she had just heard. But she hadn't heard it all. Randi told her that it wasn't until she went to her pediatrician that she was removed from her home. She was thirteen years old, and was carrying her own father's child. Gladys' head began to swim as the tears poured down her face. She began reliving her own history of child abuse and sexual molestation by members of her own family. She tried to put out of her mind the countless "coat hanger abortions" she had performed on herself; to the point that she had damaged and scarred her uterus so bad that it was impossible for her to bear her own children. She never told anyone that Charmaine was the product of Lemuel and one of her cousins; a cousin that had a crush on Lemuel and had been sleeping with him for years. Years endured watching her cousin and husband's lovemaking; the humiliation that he secretly preferred her over Gladys. Gladys was able to swallow her pride and accept the only consolation; Charmaine. Gladys; being the good church-going woman that she was, had prayed for an intervention from God that would stop those two. Charmaine came a month premature, and Hattie's husband had not yet come home from Vietnam. Charmaine was not willing to wait for Hattie to make it to the hospital. Lemuel sent Gladys to help Hattie deliver. Gladys decided to make sure that Hattie didn't enjoy having sex with Lemuel any longer.

After Charmaine was born; she gave Hattie an extra dose of sleeping powders. While Hattie enjoyed a deep, restful slumber; Gladys went to work. She knew form her own experience what she needed to do to ensure that Hattie would no longer get pleasure from any other man; nor would she be able to produce any other children. She had heard from different women around the neighborhood about 'vaginal castration' and had played dumb so that they would explain to her in great detail as to how it is performed. Not only did she cut off Hattie's clitoris; she performed a radical 'coat hanger abortion' on her. She made sure that she cut the tissue deep enough to leave huge scarring. Gladys stayed with Hattie every day while she "recuperated". Hattie complained of the immense pain she was feeling. Gladys would supply her with another "hot toddy" to ease the pain. Hattie was to find out too late that every time she would go back off to sleep, Gladys would re-scar her to make sure that she wouldn't be able to have any more children. Hattie's delivery lasted two and a half months. When she was finally better, she and Lemuel picked up where they left off. But Hattie noticed something different. She was unable to have an orgasm. Slowly; sex between she an Lemuel tapered off, until he lost interest in trying to satisfy a woman who seemed to be "unsatisfiable".   Gladys and Lemuel took care of Charmaine as their own after Hattie committed suicide.

   The next morning Gladys was awaken by the sounds coming from downstairs in the kitchen. When she made it to the top of the stairs, she was enticed by the smells of fresh cooked fried fish, grits, biscuits, and warm cinnamon. She hadn't paid attention to the grumbling in her stomach; but now it was at a full-fledged growl. The sounds of laughter and talking surprised her this early in the morning; she couldn't distinguish between any of the strange voices emanating from her kitchen.

"Mornin'; Momma." Charmaine chimed. She was tending to the fish that was on its final turn before it was ready to be drained from the fryer. It warmed Gladys' heart to see her neighbors who had rallied around her kitchen to help Charmaine prepare the "brunch". Gladys went to pick up a dish towel to pitch in and help. She was told to just sit back and take a load off of her feet; these women "had it". Gladys was offered something to drink and was waited on by Randi hand and foot. She was uncomfortable with accepting help from people; for she was accustomed to always being the one caring for other people. The "women" swarmed around her; making a fuss over her. When brunch was ready, they surprised her by escorting her out on the back porch. Charmaine and Randi had spent the night cleaning it off and getting it ready for the next morning.

They pulled out table cloths, candles and Gladys' "good" china and silverware. The women sat on the porch for several hours; eating, chatting and just enjoying each other's company. Each of the women there had something in common with each other. They had all been victims of some sort of abuse at the hands of either their husbands or a family member. They were united by a common bond; something that had initiated them into a unique and exclusive sorority. Brunch extended into dinner, and the women made a whole day of it. There were facials, manicures and pedicures, hair combing and braiding, readings, stories and a whole lot of hugging and crying. As Gladys was getting herself ready for bed, she passed by Charmaine's bedroom, and popped her head in the open doorway. She found Charmaine sitting on her bed; writing in her journal.

"Thanks for today, honey. I really needed that." Gladys said sweetly.

"No problem, Momma. We both needed it."

Charmaine replied.

Gladys lingered for a few moments; not really sure what to say next to her daughter. She didn't know what it was that she was feeling. Maybe she was feeling of gratitude for being saved from her abuser; maybe it was a feeling of finally being able to feel comfortable in her own house and not the constant worry whether or not she will anger her husband.

   Charmaine was immersed in her writing; her mind was occupied somewhere else, so she was oblivious to her mother's gaze on her. Gladys felt the warm droplet making its way down her cheek, and seeing as how she didn't want Charmaine to catch her, she slipped quietly back to her bathroom for a quiet, but long sob session in the shower. It was just what she needed instead of the glass of warm milk she was on her way to go get to help put her to sleep. She was out like a light within several minutes.

Chapter Fifteen

By the time the girls arrived back home,

things were just beginning to get hectic. Bianca had her hands full in getting Charmaine's house packed up and sent to her. She devoted all of her spare time to that task. Leslie was up to her eyeballs in negotiations with contractors over her renovations. Allison was trying to fend off the sexual advances of Reverend Willie Ray. He had set his sights on her, and had made up his mind that she was going to be his wife. His career depended on it. He was beginning to fill in for the Bishop more and more frequently. He knew that the Bishop hadn't made up his mind totally as to who his successor was going to be, either between Willie Ray or Sylvester Thalmadge. The Bishop had been utilizing these two regularly, so that he could begin the process of semi-retirement. He had been looking forward to this time in his life ever since he was ordained as a young man by his idol; the Reverend Dr.

Martin Luther King, Jr. He and his wife had it all planned out; they were to spend the first several years traveling between their children, family and close personal friends-some that they hadn't seen in decades. Then they were going to take the 2-year sabbatical exchange that the Bishop was offered for him to fill in for professors at his college alma mater. After that; it was another 3 years of lecturing and selling his books and CDs. Then; he would be ready to *fully* retire, according to the time frame they had based their plans upon. So far; though, everything was going right on schedule.

Allison was unaware that she was being included as a factor into these plans. She knew that Rev. Willie Ray was "sweet" on her; but her focus was *not* on becoming a Preacher's wife, she had set her sights on a man with much loftier "bankability". Sure; he was comfortable in helping the Reverend spend his time and money on her, but she always felt that she was not ready to commit to one man-especially not *this* man at this time. The more Allison put up resistance; the harder Rev. Willie Rae pursued her. The last thing on Allison's mind was settling down with a preacher. She had envisioned herself more of a football or basketball player's wife. She dreamed of being one of those wives whose life revolved around her husband's game schedule. She had no concept of what it took to be married to a man of the cloth.

Brenda; on the other hand, was relegating in the fact that she was busy making plans with her fiancé' Chad. She was unaware of how quickly her life was about to change. Her mind was busy planning and gathering everything that she needed for her impending wedding. For his part, Chad was tying up loose ends of his life; preparing himself to settle down as a newlywed. He was well looking forward to his bachelor party. He personally oversaw every aspect of his secretive "by invitation only" soiree. He had all of the preparations done either over the phone or over the internet. His guests were all going to meet at a common location; and then at the specified time, were all going to board a chartered plane to be flown to an undisclosed location in order to commence the festivities. Chad had requested that no gifts be bought for him; just donate the monies towards the rental of the private Island that they were going to party on. The only real stipulation that he had placed on his guests was that they leave their cell phones back home. He didn't want his guest to be encumbered with the trappings of the outside world; not on his special day. He wanted to say good-bye to his bachelorhood in his own way; he didn't want anything potentially embarrassing to come back and haunt any of his guests. Discretion was of the utmost to these types of men. These were high-class 'ballers; who could stand to lose the vast majority of their wealth (and credibility) if it ever got out as to what they were doing.

Leslie had begun to get nervous about her life with Peter up in Nova Scotia. She knew that she was *totally* not ready to spend the rest of her life in God's forsaken land. She had to think of something-*fast*!   She turned to the one person that she knew who would be able to use their contacts and influence to ensure that Peter got traded to either a team in Orlando or Miami. Sure enough, within a few weeks, Peter got a phone call that his contract had been traded several times, and that he was being traded to the new Tampa franchise that had yet to be established. He was to sit out his current contract until his new one could be finalized. Leslie didn't fully get what she wanted, but at least Peter remained close enough that he could be home on the weekends.

   With this loose end tied up, Leslie could now focus her attention on finalizing her wedding plans. A three-way wedding seemed to be in the works, with all three of them sharing the cost, instead of them having three separate weddings back-to-back-to-back. It just seemed to make good financial sense, having it all together. This way; each girl could share equally in the plans, without having to have the full financial burden heaped in her lap. When all of the parents found out about it, they were a bit relieved, also that the girls had decided to take the responsibility of the wedding on and not have their parents foot the bill. The parents; in turn, pooled all their monies together and gave the girls a one-lump sum for them to use at their discretion towards the cost of the wedding.

Chapter Sixteen

*B*ianca couldn't stop the pounding in her chest. She knew; deep in her gut, that something was definitely wrong. She just couldn't put her finger on it. Something just wasn't adding up with Caleb's story as to what happened. Her mind began to recall their history together, and the different types of situations Caleb had been in. Could she have been blind all these years not to have seen what was right in front of her? She decided that she needed to get to the bottom of this quickly; before it all blew up in her face, and she was the one left looking silly.

Initially; she had thought of recruiting her girls for this task; but decided against it. No; this tasked called for a skilled, out-of-town person who could set the trap from afar. Come in; bait the trap, and then get out of town quickly when the prey had been snared. Someone who could deliver the goods; but with no sentimental attachment involved. It came to her immediately.

She would hire a professional escort! Only; she knew that this escort had to come from a reputable modeling agency. None other models would do but the ones from "Falcon Studios".

Her first order of business was to go to one of the gay nightclubs in order to pick up "the literature", as the local gays called them. As she drove around the square, trying to figure out which club to approach; she happened across one of the newly-opened white clubs. She was certain that she could slip in and out and remain anonymous. As she suspected; not a single guy looked her way as she sauntered past the front entrance way. She was able to take her time and peruse the many different stacks of gay magazines. She thumbed through them and got a sense that they all carried the same amount of advertisement. She selected a handful and quietly made her escape back into the dark quietness of her car. As she poured over the different ads; one in particular caught her attention. It was for a masseuse/escort who just happened to have extensive porn film credentials. She knew she had found her man!

Bianca dialed the number, and explained to the person who answered the phone that she wanted to enlist a private escort for her brother, who was just coming out, but could not risk being seen out in public with another gay man. Bianca stressed that the person she wanted had to exude masculinity in every way. The person on the other end told her that the particular model that she was inquiring about may have been a bit too young; but that she may have just the person for her. Bianca had arranged to meet Tyreke the next night for cocktails, so that she could make the decision whether or not she wanted to use him; and to call back and arrange payment, if so.

The next day flew by as Bianca kept herself busy. She knew that her excitement was going to build in anticipation of meeting Tyreke. She deliberately stayed at her desk for a few minutes; for she didn't want to appear too anxious to meet him. She wanted to make sure she made a grand entrance. She took her time driving the few blocks to the restaurant. She ducked into the ladies room and "freshened up" before the meeting. She knew where in the restaurant that she was supposed to meet Tyreke, so she knew that she could take the home court advantage of scoping him out before she even decided to talk to him. She stood at the entrance of the restaurant and pretended to be waiting for her date, who was parking the car. She draped her coat over her arm; being careful to only expose the lining so that no one could tell if it were a man or woman's overcoat, and carried her briefcase by the handle (she made it a habit to carry a very masculine briefcase as a sign of shrewd business acumen), as she swung her purse over her shoulder. She asked the greeter if she could wait at the bar and order drinks until her date arrived. She knew that this ploy would give her the perfect vantage point to walk around the bar and get a full look at Tyreke without him being suspicious. Why would he? She looked like businessman's wife who was carrying around both of their belongings while he took his time to get himself together. As she suspected; Tyreke had no clue that she was scoping him out. And Bianca liked what she saw! She "accidentally" bumped his knee with the corner of her briefcase as she walked by. Tyreke proved himself to be the consummate gentleman. He offered to help her with her belongings, to order her drink, and even invited himself to keep her company while she waited. And the description that Bianca was given paled in comparison to Tyreke in the flesh. Bianca had to take pause for a moment; to remember that he was; at the very least, bi-sexual.

Damn; why the fuck are all the good brotha's on the D-L?; she thought to herself.

She had always detested the fact that black sisters were losing ground on the "good man" category, due to the fact that a lot of them were now closeted homosexuals. Bianca secretly pined for Tyreke; with his flawless, satiny blue-black skin and a set of pearly whites that looked as if god had sculpted them from pure coconut. Bianca had never seen someone whose teeth were both milky white and transparent at the same time. It was also quite obvious that he spent many a days pushing his body to its limits at the gym. His cue-ball smooth shaved head glistened as the dim restaurant lights reflected off of it.

Since Bianca had already decided on Tyreke; she decided to segue into their meeting. She introduced herself and told him that she had lost all track of time while working on an assignment, and was supposed to meet someone here. She also coyly added that her date had probably already left because she was more than fifteen minutes late. She put on her best flustered routine and gave him a look of disappointment and despair. Tyreke's face spread into a broad, toothy smile as he told her that it was probably him that she was looking for. She did the famous "valley girl" giggle with the hair toss, as she extended her hand. She knew that she had him hooked.

When Bianca left the restaurant, she had her plan well into place. Tyreke was going to do well as the perfect bait for her trap. Now; all she had to do was wait a few weeks until the holidays arrived to wait for her plan to be executed. This also gave her the critical time she needed to ensure that all of the unsuspecting players were in place to unwillingly partake of her scheme. Bianca made it easy for Caleb to let his guard down; as she increasingly made herself unavailable. She agreed to chair committees for events both at work and in the community, so that Caleb had to fend for himself. He took the bait, and began to book his calendar with extra golf and basketball games; side business trips that popped up "unexpectedly".   Bianca had primed the well…but good.

By the time the holidays rolled around, Bianca and Caleb were living two separate lives. Bianca and the girls were spending time together, yet

Caleb didn't feel threatened. Bianca began to suspect that her deepest fears were being confirmed. She figured that any way it played out, she'll get an answer. Either he will take the bait and get caught, or she'll find out that he was just that…busy with work. She would just have to sit back and let this thing play itself out.

   By the time Thanksgiving rolled around; Bianca had already set the wheels in motion. She had planned the holiday party, made plans for all of the preparations, and was now starting to get responses to the invitations that she had sent out.   She had made sure that Caleb knew well in advance what was happening, and had kept him abreast of all of her plans, step-by-step. As she suspected, he gave her carte-blanche to plan and prepare whatever she wanted to do. He promised her that he would stay out of her way; until she needed him. He didn't know how deep he was getting himself in for when he haphazardly told her; "Just tell me where to be and when to be, and I'll be there."   She knew that she had the perfect ruse. He was making himself out to be an easy patsy; only he didn't know it…yet.

Chapter Seventeen

Brenda began preparations for her upcoming spring wedding. All was in preparedness; the only thing left was to announce the engagement at Bianca's party. She knew that she was stealing Bianca's thunder, but she figured her friend would understand. She did feel a little bit bad about leaving Bianca "out of the loop", as it were. After all; this was a very important step for her to take, and she wanted her best girlfriends to share in her excitement. There were several times when she almost divulged her secret, she was so wrapped up in the revelry of the situation. She was proud of herself for being able to keep her secret for as long as she did.

She and the reverend have been in contact with each other every night for hours at a time, making plans for the future and trying to decide where they are going to live. Brenda had him research the housing market down there. She promised to come down and bring "the girls" at Easter time. Willie Ray wanted to make sure that he had his "ace in the hole" so that he made a good impression on the bishop; his future job depended on it.

Bianca couldn't stop the pounding in her chest. She knew; deep in her gut, that something was definitely wrong. She just couldn't put her finger on it. Something just wasn't adding up with Caleb's story as to what happened. Her mind began to recall their history together, and the different types of situations Caleb had been in. Could she have been blind all these years not to have seen what was right in front of her? She decided that she needed to get to the bottom of this quickly; before it all blew up in her face, and she was the one left looking silly.

Initially; she had thought of recruiting her girls for this task; but decided against it. No; this tasked called for a skilled, out-of-town person who could set the trap from afar. Come in; bait the trap, and then get out of town quickly when the prey had been snared. Someone who could deliver the goods; but with no sentimental attachment involved. It came to her immediately. She would hire a professional escort! Only; she knew that this escort had to come from a reputable modeling agency. None other models would do but the ones from "Falcon Studios".

   Her first order of business was to go to one of the gay nightclubs in order to pick up "the literature", as the local gays called them. As she drove around the square, trying to figure out which club to approach; she happened across one of the newly-opened white clubs. She was certain that she could slip in and out and remain anonymous. As she suspected; not a single guy looked her way as she sauntered past the front entrance way. She was able to take her time and peruse the many different stacks of gay magazines. She thumbed through them and got a sense that they all carried the same amount of advertisement. She selected a handful and quietly made her escape back into the dark quietness of her car. As she poured over the different ads; one in particular caught her attention. It was for a masseuse/escort who just happened to have extensive porn film credentials. She knew she had found her man!

Bianca dialed the number, and explained to the person who answered the phone that she wanted to enlist a private escort for her brother, who was just coming out, but could not risk being seen out in public with another gay man. Bianca stressed that the person she wanted had to exude masculinity in every way. The person on the other end told her that the particular model that she was inquiring about may have been a bit too young; but that she may have just the person for her. Bianca had arranged to meet Tyreke the next night for cocktails, so that she could make the decision whether or not she wanted to use him; and to call back and arrange payment, if so.

The next day flew by as Bianca kept herself busy. She knew that her excitement was going to build in anticipation of meeting Tyreke. She deliberately stayed at her desk for a few minutes; for she didn't want to appear too anxious to meet him. She wanted to make sure she made a grand entrance. She took her time driving the few blocks to the restaurant. She ducked into the ladies room and "freshened up" before the meeting. She knew where in the restaurant that she was supposed to meet Tyreke, so she knew that she could take the home court advantage of scoping him out before she even decided to talk to him. She stood at the entrance of the restaurant and pretended to be waiting for her date, who was parking the car. She draped her coat over her arm; being careful to only expose the lining so that no one could tell if it were a man or woman's overcoat, and carried her briefcase by the handle (she made it a habit to carry a very masculine briefcase as a sign of shrewd business acumen), as she swung her purse over her shoulder. She asked the greeter if she could wait at the bar and order drinks until her date arrived. She knew that this ploy would give her the perfect vantage point to walk around the bar and get a full look at Tyreke without him being suspicious. Why would he? She looked like businessman's wife who was carrying around both of their belongings while he took his time to get himself together. As she suspected; Tyreke had no clue that she was scoping him out. And Bianca liked what she saw! She "accidentally" bumped his knee with the corner of her briefcase as she walked by. Tyreke proved himself to be the consummate gentleman. He offered to help her with her belongings, to order her drink, and even invited himself to keep her company while she waited. And the description that Bianca was given paled in comparison to Tyreke in the flesh. Bianca had to take pause for a moment; to remember that he was; at the very least, bi-sexual.

Damn; why the fuck are all the good brotha's on the D-L ? She thought to herself.

   She had always detested the fact that Black sisters were losing ground on the "good man" category, due to the fact that a lot of them were now closeted homosexuals. Bianca secretly pined for Tyreke; with his flawless, satiny blue-black skin and a set of pearly whites that looked as if god had sculpted them from pure coconut. Bianca had never seen someone whose teeth were both milky white and transparent at the same time. It was also quite obvious that he spent many a days pushing his body to its limits at the gym. His cue-ball smooth shaved head glistened as the dim restaurant lights reflected off of it.

Since Bianca had already decided on Tyreke; she decided to segue into their meeting. She introduced herself and told him that she had lost all track of time while working on an assignment, and was supposed to meet someone here. She also coyly added that her date had probably already left because she was more than fifteen minutes late. She put on her best flustered routine and gave him a look of disappointment and despair. Tyreke's face spread into a broad, toothy smile as he told her that it was probably him that she was looking for. She did the famous "valley girl" giggle with the hair toss, as she extended her hand. She knew that she had him hooked.

By the time Bianca left the restaurant, she had her plan well into place. Tyreke was going to do well as the perfect bait for her trap. Now; all she had to do was wait a few weeks until the holidays arrived to wait for her plan to be executed. This also gave her the critical time she needed to ensure that all of the unsuspecting players were in place to unwillingly partake of her scheme. Bianca made it easy for Caleb to let his guard down; as she increasingly made herself unavailable. She agreed to chair committees for events both at work and in the community, so that Caleb had to fend for himself. He took the bait, and began to book his calendar with extra golf and basketball games; side business trips that popped up "unexpectedly". Bianca had primed the well...but good.

By the time the holidays rolled around, Bianca and Caleb were living two separate lives. Bianca and the girls were spending time together, yet Caleb didn't feel threatened. Bianca began to suspect that her deepest fears were being confirmed. She figured that any way it played out, she'll get an answer. Either he will take the bait and get caught, or she'll find out that he was just that...busy with work. She would just have to sit back and let this thing play itself out.

By the time Thanksgiving rolled around; Bianca had already set the wheels in motion. She had planned the holiday party, made plans for all of the preparations, and was now starting to get responses to the invitations that she had sent out. She had made sure that Caleb knew well in advance what was happening, and had kept him abreast of all of her plans, step-by-step. As she suspected, he gave her carte-blanche to plan and prepare whatever she wanted to do. He promised her that he would stay out of her way; until she needed him. He didn't know how deep he was getting himself in for when he haphazardly told her; "Just tell me where to be and when to be, and I'll be there." She knew that she had the perfect ruse. He was making himself out to be an easy patsy; only he didn't know it.

Chapter Eighteen

$\mathcal{T}$he time had finally come that Bianca had been waiting for. All those long months ago of planning and preparing had now led up to this grand fête. Bianca used her connections to get completed what needed to be done. She kept herself busy with her own project, trying to compile information on Caleb's whereabouts and dealings. She had enlisted a private detective; who had found out some sketchy information. To the best of his ability, Caleb had been keeping his nose clean and had been conducting himself on the up-and-up. Bianca; however, knew that men who were on the "down-low" did *just* that. She had a gut feeling that her feminine intuition was telling her that something wasn't right. Caleb had too many "questionable" male friends; and he always had some sort of alibi or story as to why they were always perceived as being gay. Bianca knew that there was more to it than meets the eye. And she knew that soon she would have her suspicions laid to rest.

The break she had been waiting for came a few days before the party. Caleb told her that he had to go to Atlanta to finalize a deal before year's end, or that his company stood to lose the client to their competitor. Bianca's interest was piqued. She contacted Tyreke to see what information he knew about down in Atlanta. Sure enough; he told her that he had been invited to a house party that was exclusively "by invitation only". Bianca gave Tyreke a description of Caleb and asked him to be on the lookout for him down there. She made him promise her that he would not approach Caleb and spoil her surprise; but if he could, to flirt with him to see if he would be at all interested in hooking up later. Tyreke promised and said that he would give her an update when it was over.

As agreed; Tyreke contacted her the day after the party and told her that; indeed, he had met Caleb and had agreed to come to a party as his guest. He was to bring a female as a cover, but they would arrange to meet at a pre-disclosed location later for a hook-up. Bianca's heart sank as the pit of her stomach began to wretch. It was all she could do to keep her composure and sound like the meddlesome sister. "Good; see, I knew my plan would work!" she said, as she choked on her words as they came out. She knew that what she was doing was for the best. She had to expose Caleb for using her and hiding his homosexuality behind their marriage. She was *not* going to be played for a fool by no one!

Bianca decided to drop subtle hints to let Caleb know that she was on to him. As usual; he didn't get it. Bianca's heart went cold. She felt no remorse for what was about to happen to Caleb; as far as she was concerned, he was getting what was coming to him. She sat idly by as Caleb gave her the cursory peck on the cheek as he left every morning on his way to work. Bianca downloaded "Superwoman" by Karyn White onto her I-Pod and played it incessantly in the car on her way to work. She and Caleb muddled their way through the rest of the holidays until the night of the party, when everything will all come to a head.

Bianca knew that this was going to be the night that everyone was going to talk about for years to come; and she wanted to make sure that she was flawless. Since she had taken the week off leading up to the holidays, she wanted to make sure that she had plenty of time to make herself look breathtaking on what she called her "night". She took her time relaxing and luxuriating in her tub; a pitcher of martini's at her beck and call and her private indulgence: Dunhill cigarettes. She had made a compromise with Caleb that she would only smoke at these particular times. Her own private times; like this, when she was all alone in her own private little world.

Bianca could hear the din beginning to get a bit louder, and she knew that the guests had now begun to arrive. She was more than anxious to "get the show on the road".   Caleb lightly knocked on the door and asked how long she was going to be.

"Can you be a love and keep the party going until I make my grand entrance. I'm having a problem with this vintage gown Halston delivered, but I almost have it on." She yelled towards the door. Actually; it was a lie.

 "Y'want me to try an…." Caleb began. Bianca quickly cut him off.

"No; I think I can manage. I've just got a few more buttons on the corset to do, and I'll be done." Bianca had already been dressed; coiffed and made up. No; she was using this time to text Tyreke to make sure that her plan was all set to go without a hitch. She got a glimmer in her eye when she got the message that he was just pulling into the driveway. She downed the last of her martini and then reapplied her lipstick. She took a few steps back from the mirror to get an overview of the completed package. "It's show time!" She whispered to herself as she exited her boudoir.

The party was in full swing as Bianca hit the staircase amidst "ooh's" and "ah's". Bianca knew how to work a room; and she certainly worked this one for all she could get. The girls were huddled together with their mates and as she made a bee-line for them, they all engulfed her with a sisterly embrace.

The liquor was pouring like the mighty Mississippi River, the party floor was bombarded with food trays as if it were a Roman orgy and everyone had to gorge themselves in order to keep up their strength. Bianca was waiting with baited breath for her plan to unfold. She couldn't wait until "bewitching hour", when she could sit back and watch the fireworks begin.

As the time got closer and closer, Bianca had to keep reminding herself to stay cool, calm and collected. She continually fluttered around the room, darting in and out of conversations so that she appeared to be interested in her guests, even though she had no intention of what was being said. She just wanted to be seen as being the gracious hostess. She made sure that she was seen pawing and gushing all over Caleb. Part of her plan was to appear shocked and horrified when the news broke. This way, it will seem as if she has been the one wronged. Bianca's plan was going like clockwork.

Finally; the moment had arrived. When Tyreke entered the room, you could feel the kinetic excitement increase. As Tyreke made his way through the crowd, he could sense the glare of all the eyes that were giving him the "once-over". He slowed his roll, and made sure he accentuated his swagger, thus allowing his admirers the full view of his Johnson as it batted back and forth inside his trousers. He surveyed the room, and found his mark-Bianca, holding court with a throng of party-goers. As he made a bee-line towards her, he was interrupted by a firm hand on his forearm.

"What are you doing here? Who invited you?"
Caleb asked; with a tinge of indignation.
Tyreke flashed his signature smile. By this time,
Bianca had been given the "heads-up" that
something was going on. She sauntered her way
over towards the din and chimed;
"Tyreke; how lovely of you to have made it!" She
plastered on a smile as if she was posing for the
paparazzi.
"Caleb; be a doll and take Tyreke around and
show him off to the rest of our guests". Caleb
was so flustered that he didn't catch the hint that
Bianca had just let fall like an anvil. Her trap had
been sprung. As Caleb led the way, Bianca
raised her drink (along with her eyebrow) and
sent them on their way. Bianca made her way
back to her guests as she delighted in her plan
slowly beginning to take shape.

It had been several hours, when people
began to realize that they hadn't seen Caleb and
Tyreke in a while. As the word started to spread,
the girls sprung into action of trying to find them,

for Bianca's sake. It would be several hours before anyone would see them again.

   It was in the wee hours of the morning when the guests started to leave. Bianca and the girls had begun to clean up from the party get worried when none of them had been able to locate any of them. Bianca's plan had been sprung, and now it was the time for the finale. She knew that she had to show a sense of worry and concern, so she did her best to play the part. As they searched the house; Bianca acted as if she was about to become hysterical, hinting that the boys may have been involved in foul play. She allowed the girls to work themselves into a fever pitch, all the while knowing full well was about to unfold. The moment she had waited for was finally here. There was a muffled "Oh, My God!" coming from one of the rooms upstairs. A sinister smirk crept across her face; and she knew that she immediately had to replace it with just the right sense of concern.

As the rest of the girls converged on the room, Brenda stood there; frozen like a deer caught in the headlights of an on-coming car. Each of the other four girls pushed their way into the dimly lit room, and each one stopped short. Their mouths open in aghast. This was Bianca's shining moment.

"Caleb; how could you?" She shrieked, as she went into full drama queen mode. She turned on the crocodile tears and pretended to brake down in front of everyone.

There they were; all three of them: Caleb, Tyreke and Chad all intertwined together on the floor in a ménage-a-trois. Bianca hadn't counted on ensnaring Chad in her web also, but hey…beggars can't be choosy.

Brenda had to be escorted from the doorway, as she was still in shock. Bianca was in full mock tirade mode by now. She had made sure that she had the goods on Caleb-*and* Chad. For her, it was all to deliciously wicked.

For his part, Caleb knew that it was all over. None of them had calculated the time that they had spent away from the party. They had been so engrossed in their three-some that time just slipped by them. Caleb had to face the inevitable. He knew the possibility that his marriage was over; but he was going to plead his case up to the bitter end. Charmaine and Allison were there to help clean up this messy situation. They ushered Bianca out in the blaze of arms flailing and ranting and raving, and advised the boys to get dressed. They all agreed to meet downstairs so that they could all "sort things out".

As they began to get dressed, they began to strategize about what they were going to say to compose a united front. They all agreed to back Caleb up in whatever he decided to tell Bianca. When they finally got dressed and made their way downstairs, Chad high-tailed it right out the door.

"That fuckin' coward!" Caleb snorted. Tyreke knew that he had to see this through. He had agreed to this endeavor; and had already taken the money from Bianca. He knew that she was not going to come after him; she had a bigger fish to fry. Tyreke didn't know why Bianca wanted to implicate her husband. Maybe she had suspicions that he was on the D-L, and she just wanted confirmation. Tyreke had no idea that he was going to one of his former partners and fellow Falcon Studio cast mates. Once he and Chad saw each other; the sparks once again began to ignite. Tyreke had ditched Caleb earlier on in the evening, before he had gotten side tracked with Chad. When Caleb walked in on them accidentally, things really started to heat up! Before they knew what happened, they got busted.

Chapter Nineteen

The room was eerily silent as everyone sat there, looking at each other. Bianca knew that she was totally in command of the situation. She just sat there; cool as a cucumber, feigning to be hurt and distraught. Actually, she was already planning her next move. She was shrewd and calculating. She let the girls "stew in their own juices"; as it were. Brenda had completely fallen apart over the whole thing. She kept her head in her hands; repeating:

"Why is this happening to me, Lord…why? **Why!!?**"

After about the fifth or sixth time, Bianca grew irritated with her. She was about to lose her cool with her; when Caleb cleared his throat, as if he was about to speak. All eyes diverted to him as they all waited with baited breath for something to come forth.

"…*And*?" Bianca asked; with a well-rehearsed raised eyebrow.

Caleb knew that he was not going to get out of this very easily. He had to back-peddle his way out of this situation, but he knew that he was in *waaay* too deep now.

Chapter Twenty

I had no intention on ever cheating on my wife. I had heard about those types of guys who were fed up with women, and decided to try "hookin' up" with a dude. I just never thought that *I* would be one of them; but there I was, standing at the men's counter at Dillard's Department store, being "cruised" by another dude. The bad part about it; I was actually getting quite turned on by it. It made me feel something different that I never quite felt from flirting with a woman. Dudes flirt in a totally different way than women do, I guess it was the fact that they had to keep it within certain boundaries, lest they get caught.

Usually, my wife does all of my shopping. She is the reason I have the style I have; she's the one who gave it to me. She's also responsible for the cologne I wear. I never had any time for that kinda stuff. I always had some female or another buy things for me; now, I just show my wife what I think would look good on me from the men's magazines. If my wife likes it, I'll get it. If she doesn't, I won't. The thing that got me interested in checking out the fellas was the fact that several of the more feminine ones at work would critique what I wore. They were a bit bolder than the women were; kinda like the way men are towards women. Not that I felt intimidated, but the extra attention was a bit flattering. It really piqued my curiosity to see what it was like "on the other side".

So; there I was, having this guy helping me pick out clothes to wear. First off; I was as uncomfortable as a bull in a china shop. I was *way* out of my league! But the clerk, Armand, was as patient as could be and took his time with me. He gave me some tips on the clothes that I had picked out, and why they didn't work on me. He made it his mission to compliment me on my body, and tell me that he could tell that I had been working out. Girls don't really take the time to notice things like that the way gay guys do. He knew just the right way to *"glaze"* across my crotch as he checked the inseam of my trousers at every fitting. He was careful enough not to linger there too long; just enough to get a rise out of me, and then move on. I never had a particular "type" of dude that I thought I would hook up with; I guess no one ever really does, it just happens. Armand; normally, wouldn't have caught my eye. He was too "faggy". I guess if it was going to happen, it should have been with one of my boys that I shoot hoops with. But; then again, I guess not. I couldn't see myself being as uninhibited with one of my homies, as I could with a guy that was a bit more feminine.

   After he rung up my sale, Armand thanked me profusely and flashed me the warmest smile ever...from a dude, I mean. As I took the bags from him, he slid his perfectly manicured hand across mine and whispered:
I put something "special" in the bag for you", and gave me a wink.
"Cool", I said, as I bid my adieu and made my way towards the elevators. Once in, I looked to

see how many cologne samples he had stuffed at the bottom of my bag. I fished around, but the only thing I came up with was a scented card with his digits on it. I wasn't mad at the boy, he definitely knew his game...discretion is the key.

I immediately entered the number in my celly, then tore up the card and threw it away. I couldn't leave any suspicious evidence for Bianca to find. She'd always told me about Chad, and how gullible Brenda was, so I pretty much knew how she felt about men on the D-L. I'll admit to having my dick sucked a couple of times in college, when me and my girl got into a fight, and she decided that she wasn't givin' me none. But this...this was different. Bianca and I were gellin' just fine. I don't know what made me do it. Maybe it was the "thrill of the chase". The fact that I could get away with it, and Bianca would not have been the wiser. Now; I know that we couldn't have done anything right there in the dressing rooms, I'd seen the exposés on department store video surveillance cameras in the dressing rooms. Nah…I knew better than to go that route.

   I found a pay phone in the lobby and called the number, just to make sure that it was the right one. I knew that I couldn't risk *ever* using my cell or office phone to call him. I don't want him to be able to call me back. I've heard that a lot of these guys end up calling at odd hours of the day, just to "say hi". I know I'm not interested in having them feel that it's OK to just call and talk idle "chit chat".

   Needless to say that it took several days for us to finally 'hook-up".   Armand gave me his weekly schedule, and the phone number to his station, this made it easier for me to call him. We made an arrangement to get together one afternoon that he had off, and his roommates were scheduled to work a double shift. I was able to rearrange my schedule so that we could have a few uninterrupted hours to spend together.   I also knew that we couldn't be seen together. I couldn't jeopardize having someone see me with this "nelly fag"; and then go around town blabbing. Besides, he knew what was up, he knew that it couldn't happen either. At least I *hope* his faggot ass knew it. The last thing I needed sweatin' my dick was some punk-assed faggot wanting to spend a lotta time with me. Ain't no happs.....like they say, I'm gonna hit it; then split it!

We hit it off pretty well, and I laid the ground rules down on his ass. Like I said, he knows what's up. Soon after that, I began to frequent the store more often. He gave me his employee ID number, so whenever I wanted something, I would just take it upstairs and have the customer service clerk call downstairs to Armand to verify that he was at work that day. I got a shit load of good deals on his discount. At first, every so often I would sneak in a few items for Bianca, to test the waters. Either he never saw the register receipts or he just didn't care. He never said a word. Soon, I was splurging for the both of us. I figured, what the hell, he's getting what he wants out of the deal, and I might as well get something out of it too.

It stood to reason that if I was going to get caught with as dude, most likely it should have been Armand, *not* Tyreke. I had no intentions of messing around with him, but I thought I'd remembered seeing him briefly in passing several times at Armand's job. We'd even exchanged the brotha's "hello"; the slight *tick* of the head to signal one another's acknowledgement. I was surprised to see him at Bianca's party, but had to play it off. I had no idea that he had once been kickin' it with Chad. When they saw each other, you could tell that there was some sort of chemistry between them.

At some point during the party, they managed to sneak off and started "getting' busy". I had caught them off guard when I found them, and had every intention to just let them be. It was Tyreke who enticed me to join in. I don't know what the hell I was thinking; but the alcohol got

the best of me, and the next thing I
knew...well...we *all* know what happened.

Chapter Twenty One

*I*t had been several weeks since the party, and Brenda and Chad still hadn't spoken to each other. Brenda was finding it hard to forgive Chad for what he had done. Her heart had been broken by him, and she had upheld his masculinity when everyone else was questioning it. She now knew that she had to face the truth. So, now what was she going to do? The first thing that she did was call off the wedding. She knew that deep down in her heart, she could never let him live it down. She was always going to be the one who was pitied because her husband was making a fool out of her. There was no way of escaping the truth, all of her friends were there to witness her discovery.

She had no idea how she was going to break the news to her Auntie; for she knew that her Aunt would take the news one hundred times worse than she would. All her life, her aunt had been planning and saving for this moment for as long as Brenda could remember. News like this would send her into a tail-spin. Brenda was going to have to break it to her as gingerly as she possibly could, and she was going to have to do it soon, as the wedding was only a few short months away. She and the girls had been brainstorming ideas about how she should do it, but nothing that really seemed to make any sense.

The more that Leslie and Allison prepared for their weddings, the deeper Brenda's melancholy grew. No one noticed Brenda's slow withdrawal into herself; no one except Bianca, who knew immediately that Brenda was about to become unhinged. She knew that Brenda was primed and ready to enact the next part of her plan. Now all she had to do was to add fuel to the fire to accelerate the process. At the party; they had all batted around the idea of getting together around Easter, before the wedding "deluge".

It had been agreed that they would plan to get together for a retreat during the Easter holiday.

The guys decided that they were going to rent a cabin up in the mountains, where Caleb had connections through one of his co-workers. The girls decided on something a little less adventuresome. They all agreed to spend the holiday with a sleep-over at Bianca's house. They would have a "Sex and the City" type of weekend. Bianca and Caleb agreed to supply all of the staples, the rest of that weekend was going to be whatever the girls wanted to bring, which was going to leave the field wide open.

Bianca figured that she had the perfect cover for the next phase of her plan: she used the time that she was out gathering up the supplies to contact Tyreke and give him the next steps. She was shocked when he told her that he no longer wanted any part of the rest of the plan. At first, Bianca was livid, but she decided to teach him a lesson not to cross her. All that she asked of Tyreke was to return the money that she had given him for not completing the job. She sensed that he was having remorse for crossing his one true love, Chad. A sinister smirk crept across her face as she realized what it was she was about to do. She played it all cool and close to the vest when she agreed to back off and leave him alone. Tyreke had no idea what she had in store for him!

As Chad and Brenda's relationship cooled, Chad found himself spending more and more time with Tyreke. He soon grew weary of trying to pretend to be interesting in reconciling with her. He finally had Tyreke back, after all these years of being apart. He knew that he was going to have to confront both Brenda and the rest of them at some point, but he wanted to make sure that he and Tyreke had a much more stable relationship intact before he did. He was unaware of Tyreke's secret, and only assumed that theirs was just a chance meeting…kismet as it were.

For their parts, Leslie and Allison had no clue as to the back story that was unfolding; and why should they? They had enough on their minds with the planning of their nuptials and all. Charmaine and Randi were supposed to be flying in for the wedding, and so Charmaine was *totally* out of the loop as far as disclosure was concerned. Bianca was glad of that fact, for it lent for a lot less confusion when her plan unfolded. As far as she was concerned, the less people that knew what was actually going on, the better off her plan would go without a hitch. The next several months that led up to the Easter weekend drudged on for Bianca. For Brenda; though, it was a *completely* different story. Her engagement was in a shambles, and Chad didn't seem to want to work on fixing it.

Brenda felt that if Chad would concentrate hard enough, he could overcome his "demons"; she was sure of it. So sure, in fact, that she decided to enlist her Aunt to help get him to see it her way. Brenda knew that she was going to have to tell her the whole sordid mess, so that her aunt had a clear understanding of what Brenda was facing. She knew that her aunt abided by a strong faith, which saw her through a lot of bad times. Brenda knew that if anyone was capable of helping her "heal" Chad and help him see the error of his sinful ways, it was going to be her aunt.

Brenda decided to call Chad and set up an informal meeting with him. When he balked at her choice of location, they both decided to meet in someplace neutral. When Chad showed up for their lunch with Tyreke in tow, Brenda was a bit perplexed. She brought her aunt up to speed as to who Tyreke was, and she and her aunt surmised that Chad had brought him along so that Chad could show her that he was dumping him for her. As they exchanged pleasantries, Brenda felt a bit uneasy. Chad treated her as if they were total strangers, and were meeting for the first time.

"So...who's your friend...?" Aunt Clara chimed in, as she extended her hand.

"My name is Tyreke; Ma'am". Tyreke said with all the charm of a Southern gentleman. Aunt

Clara was not impressed.

   As the waiter came around to take their order, both guys begged off. Neither of them were very hungry. Aunt Clara knew instinctively that something was not right. As Brenda ordered her food, Aunt Clara watched the two of them. She sensed the non-verbal cues and noticed immediately the lovelorn looks that they were giving each other. She knew that Chad was about to break her niece's heart, and she had to be there to pick up the pieces. She leaned over and said to the waiter, cutting off Brenda in mid-sentence, "be a love and give us a few more minutes..." she gave him a look to let him know that there was something serious going on that needed immediate attention. Food may not have been what they needed right at this particular time. The waiter scanned the foursome, and realized that Brenda was about to have her world crushed at any moment. He whisked off and left them alone. He waited with baited breath for the impending drama that was about to unfold.

As Aunt Clara prepared to get to the bottom of it all, Brenda began:

"So; Chad, I guess you've figured out by why I brought Aunt Clara along".

"No; not exactly, Bren…please enlighten me".

"Well…it's like…" Brenda began, in that "valley-girl" tone that she uses when she thinks she's being cute. Chad was not amused. Neither was Aunt Clara

"Brenda; why don't you spare us the dramatics; I don't think these gentlemen are in a particular mood for any nonsense. Aunt Clara said firmly. Brenda ignored her aunt's advice and continued on.

"I was thinking…don't you have something that you would like to tell Tyreke about…*us*? She asked, as she looked at him with a naive stare. Chad immediately grew tired of her silliness; so was Aunt Clara. She spoke up.

"You know, this meeting doesn't seem to be going well. Why don't we just take of the kid gloves and just get down to brass tacks?" She asked, as she eyeballed each one of them, as a way to say "cut the bullshit!" Which was what she really wanted to say to all of them, but was too much of a lady.

Chad and Tyreke leaned in. "We agree with you one hundred percent". Chad turned and looked directly at Brenda.

"Bren…I know that you are so in love with me; but I…" Before he could get the next words out, Brenda interrupted.

"I spoke with Bishop T. D. Jakes, and he agreed to…"

"Brenda!" Aunt Clara said forcefully through clenched teeth. She had also startled everyone by slamming her hand down on the table which made everyone jump. She couldn't believe that her niece was behaving in such a cavalier manner. She was quickly losing her patience with her.

Brenda quietly replied; "All I'm saying is…"

Aunt Clara slammed her hand down even harder; which stopped all activity in the restaurant. She raised her hand to the bridge of her nose and took a deep breath.

"Let the gentlemen speak. Please stop cutting them off, that's very rude and inconsiderate of you".

Brenda stood up from the table, threw down her napkin and grabbed her purse. "Maybe I already know what they're going to say, and I'm just not ready to hear those words come out of the mouth of the man that I love. Please allow me more time to process the fact that I have been made a fool of by the man I love, even after my friends warned me, I didn't want to believe them...silly me".

With that, she ran out towards the bathroom. There was a momentary silence as everyone sat back and took it all in.

Aunt Clara didn't say another word; she didn't have to. She excused herself from the table, laid down a twenty dollar bill and began to exit the restaurant. She knew that she wanted to go back and give the two of them a piece of her mind; to make a scene, but her sense of deportment forbid it.

Chapter Twenty Two

*B*renda retreated deeper into herself, and cut off all communication with everyone for a while. Aunt Clara understood quite well that she needed to give her niece all the time in the world to process through all that she had going on. She knew that it was going to be Brenda, and Brenda alone, who was going to determine just how long she was going to grieve. No; she knew that meddling right now was only going to push Brenda deeper into her funk.

The rest of the girls were so busy preparing for the weddings and all that they really didn't notice that they hadn't spoken to Brenda in several days. Bianca had been the busiest of them all; with coordinating the Easter retreat *and* Caleb's impending downfall. Out of everything she was dealing with, destroying Caleb was what consumed the most of her waking moments. Leslie and Allison are both in their own little worlds, both individually and collectively, that nothing else but their lives are the focus of their attention.

There was nothing else more important in their lives at this time than the wedding. Bianca had everything timed down to the split minute; she had made sure that everything went off without a hitch. Before anyone had a chance to take in a deep breath, Easter was upon them. And if there was one thing that they could count on, it was the fact that in southwest Pennsylvania, Easter in April can be quite unpredictable. You never were certain if it was going to be sunny and warm, cold and rainy or just plain frigid, snowy and icy. It was all a crap shoot. So far, it was predicted that the weather was going to remain snowy and cold, so the planning of a nice, warm retreat was just the ticket. Bianca had been well on top of things, and knew that she could relax a bit until the weekend rolled around. It was only six weeks away, and with the way things were going, time was going to fly by in the blink of an eye.

Caleb waited with eager impatience, in order to gauge Bianca's mood as to whether or not she was going to forgive him and allow him to move back in. He knew that his best option was not to push her; though, he would just have to sit tight and play it cool. The next biggest hurdle for him was that he had to face the rest of the guys for the long Easter weekend. He knew that they would be constantly judging him as to whether or not they considered him a true "brotha". There was nothing quite as demeaning as having your manhood called into question, but he knew that it had to be, he had given everyone cause to doubt it. He would just have to "suck it up and take it like a man". Between the two evils, he wasn't sure which one was the hardest to face. With every day that ticked by, he became more and more anxious. What would he do if he were to get up to the lodge and the other guys decided that they were going to 'beat the gayness out of him?' He had heard tales of such happenings; and knew the irreparable damage that could be done to his career if anyone were to ever find out what he'd done.

By the time Easter rolled around, everyone was more than ready for a break. On the ride up to the mountains, Caleb kept pretty much to himself. When asked why he was so quiet, he replied that since he was responsible for getting everyone up there safely, he was concentrating on the road. No one really could fault him for that, for the roads were pretty bad outside of the city. Much of the snow had melted in town, but the further they got from civilization and flat land, the more treacherous the terrain became. Caleb had to play it real cool, he didn't want to appear to overly cautious or insecure.

As the girls began their retreat, Bianca had made sure that they were going to do it in style. They were all picked up in a limousine and 'whisked' off to the spa. Needless to say that by the time they exited the limo, they were already "three sheets to the wind" off of Ciroc vodka imported by P. Diddy. Before long, they were all being pampered, massaged, mani/pedi-ed, and reveling in the afterglow of a pore-cleansing eucalyptus whirlpool Jacuzzi spa.

"Mmmmm…" the girls heard Bianca moan as poured herself into the steaming hot water. "This is definitely what my ass has been needing for the past several months".

"Girrrrrl….you gets an *A-MAN* from me!" Leslie replied, as she lifted up her cocktail glass in a toast.

The rest of the girls all did the same as they said in unison, "*A-MAN*!"

They spent the rest of the afternoon lounging back at Bianca's house, each girl in her own quiet respite. By the middle of the evening, they had regained their appetite, and were treated to some of the best culinary delights that Bianca's caterer had whipped up.

"Tell me what you all think of the food; because this is the caterer I have planned for both of your weddings". She announced.

"Oooooh; girrrl…." Allison began; with a mouth

full of food, "an excellent choice! "

"Glad you like it; I thought you would, he's going to do sort of the same spread for you two". Bianca replied.

Brenda didn't have much to say; she felt a bit left out. She wanted to feel a part of all of the revelry, but what could she add? All of her plans had now gone by the wayside. She began to retreat further into herself. They had all agreed that there was not going to be any talk of weddings, honeymoons, or anything like that; but now look at what happened…

Chapter Twenty Three

The guys; for their part, were not faring much better, either. Everything started out OK, but it began to get a little weird and uncomfortable quickly. To start things off, Chad and Caleb acted as if they couldn't stand each other; as if they were mortal enemies. The original sleeping arrangements had to be altered because they refused to even sleep in the same room with each other, even though the beds were across the room from each other. Then; to make matters even worse, Tyreke shows up out of the blue. Then Caleb became enraged at the thought of Chad and Tyreke sharing the room that he didn't want to sleep in with Chad in the first place. So, Caleb stormed out of the lodge in a huff.

Before things could get too far out of hand; they all decided to get some sleep before they all had to get up and go on the fishing expedition early in the morning.

"What about my man Caleb?" Tyreke asked.

"Fuck 'im!" Quipped Chad; and with that, they all retired up to their rooms.

   By the morning's early light, the boys had begun to assemble themselves outside to pack the car up to leave. Caleb was nowhere to be found.

"He must have hitched a ride back home". Peter said.

"Or, he's found another room to shack up in". Chad retorted. Since no one was in any particular mood to get into an argument that early in the morning; they all let the subject drop and went on about their day.

"So; have you two told Brenda yet that you're an item?"   Asked Peter. He wasn't asking it to be mean and catty; he was genuinely concerned with how she was handling it all.

""Yeah…we had lunch with her the other day, and broke the news to her".   Chad said; rather cavalierly. Tyreke was a bit concerned that Chad was dismissing Brenda's feelings for him as something to be ridiculed. He made a mental note to himself to check him on that later. Tyreke never had any intention on hurting Brenda, yet, she became an innocent casualty in all of this "mess".

"…And she's alright with it?" Peter asked; a bit perplexed. It just didn't seem to him like Brenda would be the type of woman who would be able to handle something like that.

"She handled it pretty well; she didn't explode, or break down and cry, or any of that, did she Tyreke?"

"No…she didn't.…" Tyreke began.

"She just got up and walked out. Left us just sitting there with our mouths open". Chad interjected.

Tyreke knew what was happening. Chad wasn't telling the full story for a reason. He knew that he was going to look like a heel; and he wanted to get in good with them, before Brenda could smear his name. Tyreke knew full well that his plan could blow up in his face; but he said nothing of the contrary. He realized that this was going to be Chad's mess to fix and clean up, not his. He soon began to ask himself a fundamental question: If Chad was capable of treating Brenda with such disregard, what would prevent Chad from treating him the same way? Tyreke suddenly felt a twinge of contempt for Chad; as he was beginning to sense that Chad was an "opportunist". He had the nagging feeling that Chad was only looking out for Chad; no one else, and would do anything to ensure that his own wants and needs were fulfilled. Everyone else's be damned.

Tyreke felt it was in his best interest to just sit back and watch Chad this weekend, just to see how he handled himself with the rest of the guys. Then; for some unknown reason, his thoughts turned to Caleb. Why *did* he storm out last night? What had been going on between him and Chad that would make him behave that way? Why did Chad seem to be so pissed off when

Caleb was discussed? Tyreke began to get a sense that there was more to them two than just acquaintances. Then it hit him: Bianca *knew* that he alone was the point man to bring out the worst in her husband. Bianca already had suspicions that something was happening between Chad and Caleb, she just needed someone to come in between the two of them so that they can bicker and tear each other apart. Then she could appear to be the jilted woman and take Caleb to the cleaners.   A smile crept across Tyreke's face as he realized that he now had leverage in Bianca's game. He'd figured it all out. The rest was going to be like taking candy from a baby.

   Tyreke decided that he was going to play "double agent". He was going to go along with this little charade. He would secretly make a deal with Caleb against Chad by agreeing to tell him everything he knew. So; Caleb would pay Tyreke to sleep with Chad, while Tyreke fed Caleb information to bust Chad's shit wide open to Brenda. Brenda would then be so grateful, that she would finally know the whole truth. Chad would be busted; and would break it off with him; thereby leaving him with nothing and no one; as he and Caleb are no longer speaking to each other.

Bianca would have gotten rid of Caleb, and then Caleb would be free. Hopefully, he would remember the good time they had together, and would be amenable to begin seeing each other. He knew that it was very tricky and complicated, and had to be handled with the utmost finesse. The big test would be what happens when they returned to the lodge and reencounter Caleb again.

When they returned to the lodge, it was just as they had left it earlier that morning. There was no visible signs that Caleb had ever been there. "We'd better call him to make sure that he is OK". Peter said.

"I agree". Tyreke added.

"What the hell for? If he wants to behave like

some silly-assed schoolgirl, then let him. I ain't gonna be chasin' after no grown man like some bitch!" Chad snapped.

"Man; you need to check yourself, if it wasn't for Caleb, we wouldn't even be up here in the first place. An' you gon' just say 'Let him go? If it were you; would you want us to just ignore you?" Willie Ray said.

"First of all; I wouldn't fly out of here; all in a huff like a fuckin' bitch!" Chad began.

"STOP IT; both of you!" Tyreke bellowed. It scared the shit out of everyone, and they all froze dead in their tracks.

"This stupid tit-for-tat isn't getting us anywhere. We all came up here as a group; we're all leaving here as a group. Period. End of story". None of them had ever seen this side of Tyreke before. He took command of the situation and gave everyone a chore to do. Chad grumbled and complained about his; but he was a bit afraid to cross Tyreke at this point. He wasn't even concerned that another human being was unaccounted for, and had been unaccounted for, for quite some time.

Tyreke took the task of calling Bianca to see if Caleb had contacted her yet. Bianca told him that it was just like Caleb to go off and be by himself like that, and not to worry. He'll be back when it was time to leave. She seemed unfazed when he told her why he flew off the handle; although he still was a bit perplexed at how calm she was.

"Tell you what..." she finally said; "If he isn't back an hour before you guys are ready to leave to come home, *then* I'll begin to get worried". Tyreke found that to be a bit strange. There seemed to be no caring for her missing husband. No concern if he wasn't lost somewhere in a ditch. He found her lack of love for him to be disheartening.

They spent the rest of the three day weekend really taking the time out to get to know each other; and they realized that Tyreke was a stand-up kind of dude. Chad was the one who turned out to be a bit flaky. He was moody and pouty the whole weekend; just an all-over wet blanket. Nothing they did or said went over well with him. Tyreke often ignored him and left him alone to brood all by his lonesome.   And as Bianca had said, Caleb returned the night before they were ready to leave.   He just walked in; happy as you please, as if he'd only been gone for a few moments.

"Man…where the hell have *you* been!?" Barked Tyreke.

"Now, you're my mother all of the sudden. Relax…I'm a big boy. I can take care of myself. Besides, you forget that I have been coming up here for years…remember? I know my way around these parts".

"Yo; dude….you had us worried". Peter said. Caleb was surprised to see the hurt look in his eyes. He never knew that a brotha could care that much about another brotha's well-being. It really touched his heart that these two guys actually gave a damn whether or not he was

alright. He hadn't counted on that. He really felt
as if he'd let them all down. He wasn't used to
this. Bianca *never* made a fuss over him. Neither
did his parents. He'd always felt alone in this
world, and that no one ever really cared about
anyone else. He was proven wrong. It had
touched his heart.

"Guys…I am *really* sorry. I don't know what else
to say. Sorry if I ruined your weekend". Was all
he said; quietly. They all came over and hugged
him; everyone except for Chad, that is. He sat
on the couch, brooding as usual. The rest of the
night the guys sat up, ran the dozens on each
other, finished off the rest of the beer and played
poker. Chad had long gone upstairs to bed by
himself.

   The ride home fared much better for Caleb
than it did on the drive up. He and Chad still had
not cleared the air, and he was not exactly sure
why he was now behaving like a spoiled bitch.
He got what he wanted; he and his "lover" were
accepted by the rest of the guys, and they

enjoyed a nice little "romp" free from Brenda's scrutiny. The way he figured it, Chad had no reason at all to be pissed off. There was an interesting break in Chad's behavior. At one point during the ride home, Caleb let his mind wander off in the distance. He wasn't paying too much attention to anything, and just happened to glance up in the rearview mirror. He was shocked to see Chad staring straight back at him; and it actually made him nervous.

   For the rest of the ride home, they played this cat-and-mouse game with each other, which both exhilarated and confused him. He wasn't quite sure what it was that Chad was expecting out of him, which didn't sit well with him. He wondered if Chad wanted to continue to have a relationship with him now. (He was well aware that some guys prefer dating other guys who are already in relationships, but he wasn't one of them). He *almost* considered making a play for Chad, but stopped when he thought of the consequences that it might cause. He wasn't sure if he could trust Chad. There was just something that just didn't sit well with him. So, he decided to just let it drop.

Whatever it was that he was thinking about getting into wasn't worth the risk if he would have gotten caught. Besides, he already was on thin ground with Bianca, the last thing that he needed was to do something else to give her a reason to divorce him and take his ass to the cleaners. It would have been as if he'd cut off his own head and served it to her on a silver platter. He had much to much to lose at this point, he knew that he definitely didn't want to flush it all down the tubes. Especially over a simple flirtatious glance in the rearview mirror. Now, that would have just been plain silly, something that one of those silly-assed faggots who professed their undying love for him do.

Although it was a tad ass-backwards, Caleb dropped Chad and Tyreke off first. He wanted to make sure that no one could say that the three of them were last seen together, in case some shit just happened to get stirred up. On his way back to his hotel room, he made sure to stop by the house and see if Bianca was home. He wanted her to see that he was trying his best to prove to her that he wasn't doing anything to jeopardize their getting back together. It was just his luck that she was standing at the front doorway, saying goodbye to Allison. He pulled into the driveway, and walked up to greet them.

"'Evenin', ladies". He said, as he turned on his most genteel Southern charm. Allison giggled and waved him goodbye as they passed each other in the walkway.   Bianca; however, was another story. She stood there with an icy cold stare.

"Can I help you?" She said; icily. Caleb leaned in to plant a kiss on her cheek, but she threw up her hand to stop him.

"*Like…I…said…**how may I help you!**?*" This time, her voice took on a much sterner tone. Caleb was taken aback.

"*What…* can't I give you a kiss hello anymore?"

He asked; feeling a bit put-out. He was starting to get pissed off.

"Don't forget…you're still my wife. Or have you already fuckin' some other niggah already!" Anger was getting the best of him, and he was beginning to become un-done. Bianca could sense the heated electricity in the air; and decided to go for broke.

"Actually; I took a page out of your book…I just got finished eatin' the hell out of Allison's pussy. Why do you think she bounced out of here with such a big smile on her face?" She gloated. It did the trick! Before either of them knew what happened, Caleb had punched her square in her mouth, and blood began to fly everywhere as she fell over backwards into the house. Caleb was on top of her quick as a flash, tearing at her clothes as she began screaming and flailing about.

"Bitch; you think that shit is funny, huh?" He hissed in her face.

"I'll show you how funny it is!" And with that, he

tore off her panties, undid his fly, and began pounding on her as if they were in some low-budget porn movie.

"Fuck....you...bitch...I'm...still...your... husband....!" He huffed out loud with each thrust. Bianca tried to fight him off; but the more she struggled; the harder he pressed her. The attack seemed to last forever. Before she lost consciousness, she could remember hearing the blare of sirens and the flashing of lights.

Chapter Twenty Four

The ensuing months following Bianca's ordeal with Caleb left her enraged with him. She became consumed with exacting revenge against him. The very first thing that she did was file a protection from abuse for domestic violence request against Caleb. The hearing was set for after the wedding, which more than pissed her off. She wanted Caleb locked up; but he wasn't, which further infuriated Bianca. She then decided that she needed to do something drastic before the hearing so that she could bury him in court. Thank goodness the judge had the smarts to prohibit him from being within her immediate vicinity until after the hearing.

Bianca then decided to request security guards, at his expense. The judge summarily denied it. She then enlisted her friends to ensure her safety. They tended to her around the clock, screened her calls, and pampered her as if she were a celebrity. Brenda felt a twinge of jealousy. Here she was; the one who was wronged and humiliated publicly, yet Bianca manages to have all this fuss made over her. Brenda didn't see the justice in it.   All that did was make Brenda retreat further into herself. Things just *had* to start to get better; she didn't know how much more she could take.

   The eight short weeks leading up to the wedding were both tumultuous and chaotic. Caleb posted bail, and was warned to stay away from Bianca. Brenda stepped up to the plate and fill in for Bianca while she was on the mend. It was Brenda who coordinated all of the final fittings, floral arrangements, music rehearsals, wedding shower, and rehearsal dinner. It was she who was the one acting as the "wedding planner".   It was kooky, country, backwards, naïve Brenda who kept it all together during this hectic time. Brenda threw herself into it head-first, and expended all of her energies, in order to divert her attention from her crumbling personal life. Having the chance to run around town, picking up the deliveries personally gave her a sense of purpose. Not having to have Chad on her mind every moment of the day felt *very* good. It also gave her a chance to pop in and check up on Bianca, just to see how she was feeling, and to check in with her as to any last minute details she may have forgotten. It was Brenda who was there when Bianca was ready to be discharged from the hospital. She took on the added responsibility of arranging her visiting nurses and coordinating all of her legal affairs.

Brenda was thankful to have a distraction to take her mind off of Chad and Tyreke. It was also interesting that Caleb was beginning to talk to her. She knew that the only reason he was was so that he could keep tabs on Bianca. Brenda wanted to get as much information out of him about Chas as *she* could. The two of them did this "dance" with each other; both of them trying to feel each other out as to how much the other knew.   It took up a lot of Brenda's time, and before long the wedding was only a few weeks away. Brenda was looking forward to fulfilling the task that she had taken up upon Bianca's incapacitation; but was informed the night before the rehearsal dinner that her services were no longer required. Bianca was insisting that she was feeling better; and that she was going to officiate at the dinner, Brenda once again felt put-out.

There were many feelings that Brenda felt as she hung up the phone: insulted, betrayed, enraged, hurt, disappointed. She fought back the flood of tears that were welling up from deep inside of her. She decided to take matters into her own hands and go for a drive. Nothing too serious, just a drive around by the beach to get the salt air into her lungs and clear her mind. Why was she always the one that people shit upon? Why didn't people take her feelings into account? Why wasn't she taken seriously? The more she thought about these things, the angrier she became. The drive to the beach got diverted by the strip mall. She decided that she needed to pick up a few things to get her mind off of what she was now feeling.

"Looks like you're gonna have yourself a little celebration…" The cashier said to her as she rang up her purchases.

"Yeah; I have a couple of weddings to go to in a few weeks, and couldn't decide what to get. This way, I can make baskets and be done with it all." She chimed.

"Now…that's a good idea; I think I'm gonna steal your idea. Oh wait…is this yours?" The cashier asked.

"Yeah; I need to put this in my car, it's leaking fluids", Brenda replied.

Brenda felt a certain sense of calm overtake her as she leisurely made her way home. Soon, it was all going to be over, and she would be able to get on with her life. She had been working on a surprise for all of her friends, and had planned to "spring it on them" then. She began to work feverishly on the baskets, with a renewed sense of confidence that they would be well appreciated by her friends as a lovingly, thoughtful gesture. She put aside the evil thoughts that tried to creep into her brain as to the hurt and pain that she had been dealt when she was told that she was no longer wanted. When they saw these gifts, they would all feel sorry for pushing her aside. No one else was going to take the time to custom pick and hand-wrap every single item.

While everyone else was relishing in the festivities leading up to the day of the wedding, not one of the girls even realized that Brenda was nowhere around. It was as if she didn't even exist in their world at that point. Brenda waited with baited breath for the phone call from any one of the girls that she had been missed. Nothing was forthcoming. It told her all that she needed to know about how they actually felt about her. She wasn't going to make a scene at the reception; no, she decided that she actually wasn't even going to go. She would have the baskets hand delivered, and would be long gone

by the time they were away on their
honeymoons.

Chapter Twenty Five

The morning of the wedding had finally arrived. There was really nothing for anyone to do; Brenda had made sure of that. All of the many parts just fell into place, just as she had orchestrated. Everyone knew the part that they had to play; Bianca showed up with nothing to have to do except look exquisite and take the credit for it all. Brenda had not been given the rightful credit that she had deserved, but as Bianca saw it, no one had ever expected Brenda to be able to accomplish anything of this magnitude anyway. It was well known that it was Bianca, not Brenda, that had the polish and connections. Hell, Brenda couldn't even manage her own life, let alone someone else's! Bianca was not going to allow this "country bumpkin" steal her thunder; no way in east/west hell! She took her place in the church hall, directing traffic as if she were Leona Helmsley herself; accepting the accolades for pulling everything off; especially in her condition.

Bianca plastered on her most phony, saccharine smile, and waved them off as if she was too busy to pay any attention to them. As the rest of the guests arrive, Bianca pawned them off onto one of the junior attendants. She went and sat herself front-and-center in the front pew; the one reserved for family.

As rehearsed, the wedding went off without a hitch. The church was full of well-wishers, family and friends. Bianca was *supposed* to coordinate the wedding reception also; but she delegated *that* task to another junior attendant also. Brenda showed up during the transition from the wedding to the reception. She noticed that she wasn't the only one who was just arriving. She enlisted the help of some of the male ushers to help her bring in the baskets. As she and the other party go-ers began to fill the reception hall located behind the church, she noticed Caleb's car pull in. The nuptials were wrapping up, and she knew that the newlyweds would be exiting shortly. She also knew that since it was a double wedding; that it was going to take some time for everyone to gather everything together and get all parties involved together for pictures and the throwing of the rice, so she knew she had a few precious moments to spare.

"What are you doing here; you want to get arrested?" Her tone was a one of concern; not consternation. She could smell the liquor oozing out of Caleb's every pore.

"That bitch wants to ruin me!" He shouted, as he stumbled out of the car.   Brenda had to think; and think quickly. Fortunately, her prayers were quickly answered. Just then, Chad and Tyreke pulled into the parking lot. She flagged them over to her.

As they pulled up, they could both sense that something was wrong.

"What's going on?" Chad asked, as they both looked up at her from the open convertible.

Brenda didn't have to go into it; Caleb was stammering around and spitting out obscenities. "What do you want us to do?" Chad asked; a bit indignantly.

"….Nothing; never mind, I got it." Brenda said.

As Brenda stood there; contemplating her next move, she instantly thought of just hopping back in her car and getting the hell out of Dodge. She decided that it was the best plan. Let them deal with it. They didn't realize that she wasn't involved in anything else, why should she help them now?

She was just about to pull out of her parking spot when something caught her eye. *Did she just see what she thought she saw?* She backed out a few inches more and adjusted her rearview mirror to get a clearer view. No; her eyes hadn't deceived her. Chad and Tyreke were embraced in a long, drawn out kiss, right there in the parking lot! Her heart sank. Her mind began to flood with images and emotions. She didn't know what to think next. Her life was crashing all around her, and she wasn't sure as to what to do next. She pulled the rest of the way out of the parking stall, and tore out of the lot. She knew that she needed to get away and gather her thoughts. To hell with the rest of them; let them all deal with the mess that was about to jump off. She didn't know why Chad felt that he had to be there. Wasn't what he had put her through enough!

Soon, the reception is in full swing. There are so many more guests that have arrived, that it spills out onto the yard. Caleb manages to keep a low profile, as do Chad and Tyreke. Caleb catches a glimpse of Bianca, and begins to follow her as she makes her rounds through the party crowd. Soon, comes the time when the toasts begin. As everyone gathers around, Caleb makes sure that he lingers in the back so that he doesn't get spotted. He is unaware that Chad and Tyreke have already tipped Bianca that he was there, and she sends out some bouncers to ensure that he is ejected.

"I think they're looking for you; you better get outta here". He hears; whispered in his ear. As he whips around, he is greeted by a smiling cater waiter, holding a tray of empties.

"Thanks..." he says; quietly, as he looks around for an exit strategy.

"....but first there's something I need to do". He says, as he makes his way towards the kitchen area. He places a plain, white envelope in the hands of the maitre 'd and instructs him to deliver it to either of the grooms; and then he quietly slips off, with the help of the waiter.

As instructed, the maitre'd hands off the envelope to one of his staff, who makes a bee line directly to the wedding party. Peter opens the envelope, and stands up to read its contents:

I never meant for things to turn out like this
All I ever wanted was someone to love me
And accept the fact that I am a man with needs
Someone who was able to accept me with all of my faults
As I was able to accept her with all of hers

But I can see that it is no longer possible
So, now I must go, go and find my own way in this life
Everything that I have has been taken away from me
And your love for me has vanished
I can never undo what I have done
So what's the use in even trying?
I hope you all have a wonderful life together
And I hope love works for you
For it didn't for me.

Everyone then starts looking around to see if they can spot Caleb, but soon realize that he is nowhere to be found. The maitre 'd confessed that once the letter was placed in his hands, he watched as Caleb high-tailed it out into the parking lot, and sped off in his car.   Soon; everyone forgot about Caleb and got back to their revelry-making.

"Excuse me; I'd like to make a toast…"   Brenda's voice wafted over the PA system. Everyone stopped dead in their tracks as she made her way down to the center of the dance floor; with her fingers gingerly interlaced amongst three champagne flutes. She sauntered her way over to Chad and Tyreke, who looked shocked to see her coming towards them. She extends her hands, and they each take a glass from her. "This is a time for love, and a time for old loves to let go so that new love can blossom. Sometimes, we hold onto the ones we love so tightly, afraid that no one will ever love us, that we don't see that our love is not what the other one wants. I propose a toast to one such love...my Chad; that I; too, held on for too long. I didn't want to believe that you didn't love me as much as I loved you, but now I know that I could never hold onto you. I wish the two of you all the best in the world. I hope your love withstands the test of time".   And with that; they all lifted their glasses. Chad and Tyreke felt finally free to express their love for each other publicly, as they embraced and kissed openly for the first time.

Brenda put her glass down, and hugged both of them tightly. She sobbed quietly on their shoulders as she released the last of her lover for Chad. She said not another word. She politely and discretely dismissed herself.

"Where'd she go?"   Leslie leaned over and whispered to Bianca.

"Probably in the 'loo to fix her face... I hope". Bianca said; feeling a bit upstaged. No one saw neither hide nor hair of Brenda the rest of the evening; nor did anyone seem to notice that she wasn't even there.

Chapter Twenty Six

*B*ianca was awakened out of a sound and peaceful sleep by a thunderous rapping at her front door. No matter how hard she tries to ignore it, it doesn't stop. She is finally jolted out of bed by the blasts of the police sirens as they wail outside her window.

"...Now what!?" She grumbles; as she fumbles around to find her robe and slippers. The knocking intensifies.

"Hold on; I'm coming...***Dammit!!***" She shrieks.

"....what in the....!!!?" She begins as she flings open the door. She stops in mid-sentence, as she notices the bevy of squad cars lining her driveway, and the sheer force of patrolmen now stationed at her front door.

"Excuse me, Ma'am..." The policeman began.

"...yes?" Bianca replied. She knew that she had to feign ignorance in order to ensure that her reaction of shock and surprise appeared to be genuine.

"It's safe to assume that you're Mrs. Malloy…Mrs. Caleb Malloy?"

"Yes; but it's actually Bianca *Paxton-Malloy*." She corrected; with and air of haughtiness, as if she was offended that he wouldn't have retained her maiden name. The officer either had never experienced this type of woman before, or he chose to ignore her response.

"Sorry about that Mrs. Paxton-Malloy…"

"That's quite alright officer…how can I be of service?" She asked, as she stood there in the doorway, doing her best to look confused and disoriented.

"Just a few questions; if we may…?" The officer queried.

"Sure; please come in…" Bianca said, as she swung open the door and motioned for them to enter.

"Have I done something wrong?" She began, as she made her voice begin to quiver, as if she was about to cry.

"No; no Ma'am, not at all. There's been a serious accident…" the officer began. On cue, Bianca immediately clutched her hand up to her mouth and began her routine.

"**Oh my God!** Is everything alright? Who? When…?" She began as the cued tears began to fall.

'Ma'am; you may want to sit down for this…"
One of the officers stated, as he moved in closer to her.

As instructed; Bianca sat down, and in her best rehearsed theatrics, she showed her most distressed look.

"It appears that your husband was involved in a fatal car crash. There were no survivors". The lead officer began.

"***Survivors!?***…how many people were in the car with him?" Bianca said; now genuinely in shock, she hadn't expected this. For all she knew, everyone had been accounted for; she had personally seen everyone to the door as they left the reception. Then it hit her. Caleb had either picked someone up later on, or had arranged to meet someone. She had to work hard in order to contain the sinister smirk that was attempting to spread across her face.

Cool it….we don't want to blow our cover! She thought to herself.

"It appears that Mr. Malloy had given a ride to one of the waiters at the affair he had attended last night. They apparently were traveling at excessive high speeds, and Mr. Malloy either lost control of the wheel or swerved to avoid something in the road. Either way, he was unable to correct his mistake in time, and they flew over an embankment. His Mercedes was discovered upside-down just a few short hours ago. Unfortunately, both passengers were crushed to death on impact.

Bianca hadn't expected to feel the sudden emotions that she was now feeling. What she first thought was going to be relief, overjoyed, vindication, now gave way to something that she was unable to put a finger on.

"Ma'am, I have to ask a very embarrassing and complicated question…" the officer continued. Bianca looked up at him blankly.

"How well did you *know* your husband?" He began; as he was visibly uncomfortable about the subject he was about to broach with her. Bianca made sure that her face contorted in such a manner that she had to force him to divulge all of the whole, sordid details.

For the police officer's part; he was floundering like a fish out of water. One of the junior officers spoke up and took the lead.

"Did you have any reason to suspect that your husband may have been bi-sexual?" He asked. Bianca lowered her head and began to sob her crocodile tears.

"I had suspected that he was having an affair. When I confronted him about it, he of course denied it. That's why he moved out and into the apartment". She sighed.

The police officers looked at each other with a look that they give when they have a suspect that they believe has just incriminated themselves. "Did you know about these?" The lead officer asked; as he handed her a stack of photographs. "We found these at the scene of the accident. It appears that he'd been blackmailed".

Bianca was surprised at seeing them. She had been told by Tyreke that he was uncomfortable about taking such incriminating photos; so he wasn't going to do it, but now she had the actual proof that she had wanted. She then assumed that these had been taken by the private investigator that she had just hired, but the dates were from several months ago. Now, though, it was all a moot point. Caleb was dead. This was not now she had planned for it to end. She took a minute to soak it all in. It was too much for her to hope for. Caleb was dead after all, she didn't have to go through a messy divorce, and she inherited everything; no questions asked. She was now a wealthy widow!

"Ma'am…?" The officer asked, as he snapped her out of her revelry.

Bianca was so engrossed with the photos that she didn't hear him at first.

"Ma'am…?" He asked again, a bit more forceful.

"Where did you get these?" She asked, as she finally gazed up at him.

"They were strewn all about the accident scene. They apparently fell out of the trunk during the subsequent fall down the embankment".

"…oh…" Bianca said quietly, almost even silently to herself. She made sure that she looked at the pictures with disbelief; when actually it was with disgust. There; splayed in front of her, was her husband, Chad and Tyreke, in various compromising sexual situations. Bianca was shocked to see her husband being sodomized by both Tyreke *and* Chad. She had always assumed that; if anything, the most that he would have done was to have had his dick sucked. There it was; staring her in her face, her husband getting fucked by Tyreke while he was sucking off Chad! Her stomach wretched as she thought of how many times they had engaged in this activity. Then; the realization hit her that Caleb had raped her, wanting to assert his masculinity. She began to dry heave.

"Ma'am; are you alright?   I understand how disturbing they must be".   The lead officer said; as he reached out to take the pictures from her. One of the other officers had gone and found a box of tissues, and gave them to her.

"Thank you". She sobbed, as the officer's tried to get her to focus on them.

"Where is his body?"   Bianca asked, in between sobs. This was the question that the officers had dreaded, but knew was inevitable.

"They were crushed beyond recognition. We were only able to piece several things together based on the fact that articles were ejected from the car before it came to rest at the bottom of the embankment". The officer stated. "We are going to have to have the coroner check the dental records to make a positive I.D." He stated.

Bianca nodded her head in comprehension.

"So; what do I do now?" She inquired.

"Do you know who might have taken these?"
The lead officer asked, as he held the photos out,
and shook them.

"I'd be lying if I didn't tell you that I'd hired a P.I.
to trail him to see what he was up to, but by the
looks of these pictures, someone else had
already beaten me to the punch. I'd have to
admit
I wouldn't be surprised if Brenda didn't do it".
She added.

    She threw the officers for a loop. As they
pulled out their notepads, Bianca began to tell
them how she and the other girls had their
suspicions about Chad from the beginning, and
had expressed their concerns to her but was
rebuffed. She then went on to tell them about
how they had caught them in the act several
months prior. She was careful not to divulge that
it was her introduction of Tyreke in the first place
that initiated the whole chain of events. That's

when she realized that Tyreke could blow her story out of the water. She told herself that she was going to have to get a hold of him and broker a deal to keep him quiet. After a few more questions and clarifications of names, places and events, the police officers concluded their investigation with her. Before they left, the lead officer gave her his card and asked told her that someone was going to be contacting her with the outcome of the coroner's inquest.

   As Bianca gathered her wits about her as to what to do about Tyreke, she decided to do some damage control. She immediately got on the phone and began to call Brenda. After several attempts to contact her, she gave up and decided to contact everyone else that she thought would help bolster her alibi as the "jilted wife".   Person after person, she connected with answering machines. She soon realized that everyone else was probably still sleeping off their party-going from last night. She was certain that her distressful message of Caleb being killed would get her phone ringing off the hook once everyone woke up and check their voice mails. She then did the next best thing: she contacted both she and Caleb's parents. *That* got the morning off to the races!

Chapter Twenty Seven

*F*or the next several hours, she was fielding phone calls from both sides of the family. She repeated the story dozens of times, over and over, till she was tired of it. As predicted; both sets of parents were going to make arrangements to fly down for the funeral. Mama Malloy took the news exceptionally hard; as was expected. Bianca was surprised to learn that his parents had known for a while that he was gay. And not from his parents, either. His auntie had spilled the beans accidentally with the comment; "I knew that it was only going to be a matter of time before he showed his true colors to you". When Bianca asked her for an explanation, she broke down and told her how the family had an inkling that there was something different about Caleb at a young age; but his father made sure that he kept it in check. She had known that he had been secretly seeing guys, but was bringing females around as a smokescreen to keep up appearances to his parents.

With each sentence that Caleb's aunt spoke, Bianca realized more and more that she was just as naïve as Brenda was. How could she have not seen the warning signs? How did she not know that her man was *also* on the Down-Low, just like Brenda's? What was it about the two of them that attracted those types of men? She thought that she had been careful to make sure that she pre-screened Caleb to ensure that there was nothing suspect with him; how did she miss it? She became angry with herself for not having been able to see past his rouse.

Before long, Bianca's phone was ringing off the hook, with people breaking into her calls with one another, getting updates on what was going on. She was now getting the attention that she had intended. As expected, everyone sprung into action, offering their assistance in her time of need. She, of course, agreed to allow them to fulfill their duties. She was, after all, the grieving widow…

Bianca was surprised when Aunt Clara contacted her and asked if she'd heard anything from Brenda. Bianca relayed that she'd tried to contact her, but had been unsuccessful. They both agreed to give her a couple more hours to sleep before they would meet and drive over to check up on her. They both agreed to be there when they broke the news to her about Caleb. Before long, well-wishers began to arrive, bearing food and moral support. Bianca was in her glory, as she sat back and allowed herself, once again, to be pampered.

Chapter Twenty Eight

*I*t had only been a few hours since he had
been there; but this time, the junior officer who
had asked her about Caleb's bi-sexuality was
once again standing in her living room.

"Mrs. Mal...pardon; Mrs. Paxton-Malloy, I hate to
bother you at a time like this; but would you be so
kind as to accompany me..." and then he got a
call over his walkie-talkie.

"Excuse me...I'll be right back. May I? " He
asked.

"Please, help yourself ..." Bianca replied, as she
extended her arm towards the kitchen.

As the officer made his way towards the kitchen,
Bianca was swarmed with inquiries. She fielded
all questions to the best of her ability, as she tried
to keep an ear on what was going on with the
officer. After a few brief moments, the officer
returned with a sense of urgency in his gait. He
explained that there was a disturbance over at
Chad's house, and he'd just been summoned

there. And with that, he excused himself, and was gone in a flash. Once again, Bianca returned to the drones that were buzzing around her.

The scene at Chad's house was abuzz with activity. The police had gone to question Chad and Tyreke about the photos, and were alerted by a dog that was apparently barking and whining in distress. They had contacted the building superintendent, who had let them in. They found them both laying side-by-side in various forms of undress, dead. The coroner's inquest had already begun, and now the police were beginning their investigation. By all accounts, it appeared to be a double suicide, as nothing seemed to be out of the ordinary. They were all just about to exit the apartment, when an envelope lying in a stack of mail on the kitchen counter caught the junior officer's eye.

"Hey, Sarge…check this out…." He said, as he pointed to the package.

"What is it?" The lead officer said, as he made his way over towards him.

"I dunno; something about this package just caught my attention. It's the same type of envelope as the one we found near the car". The junior officer replied.

As the lead officer paid careful attention not to touch anything, he sifted through the stack of mail with his pen until he came to the overstuffed Manila envelope. Sure enough, the handwriting was exactly the same as the one that they found near Caleb's accident. It had two words only, just like the other one:

For You

. It had already been opened, and then resealed, but as they attempted to move it to be bagged as evidence, its contents spilled out of it onto the floor. Just like the officer had wanted it to. This time, a handwritten note was discovered along with the photos. A forensic investigator was called out to gather the evidence in order to determine its originator.

Needless to say that Bianca was now considered a prime suspect. "Let's go over to

Ms. Goins' home, and see if she can shed some light on this subject". The lead officer stated; and took a contingent of officers with him. En route to Brenda's house, central dispatch contacted him and told him that Aunt Clara was going to be waiting outside of Brenda's for them. She had contacted the police department, requesting their help, as she hadn't heard from Brenda for a while and was concerned. She told the dispatch operator that she had concerns about Brenda and Chad. And in light of what Bianca had told her about Caleb; her female intuition told her that something just wasn't sitting right with her. The police were more than eager to meet with her.

Aunt Clara was pacing up and down Brenda's driveway, waiting frantically for the police to arrive. She almost got herself run over by them, as she ran out into the street to meet them when she saw them rounding the corner.

"Thank God you're here...I just know something awful has just happened to her, it's not like her not to talk to me for several weeks like this".

Aunt Clara said, hurriedly. The lead officer wasted no time garnering as much information from her as he could; and was glad that she had a spare key, so that they didn't have to waste time getting a court order. They wanted to go in alone, but Aunt Clara insisted that she go in with them. Since things were already tense, and Aunt Clara was not giving up the key unless she accompanied them, their hands were tied. In they all went.

Aunt Clara was the first to find her, eerily lying there dead in a bed that was made up like a bridal coffin. Brenda had returned home from the party; changed into a wedding ensemble and had taken her own life, somehow. It was now clear to Aunt Clara that her niece had been deeply troubled by the recent chain of events surrounding she and Chad's break-up. It became all too apparent that Brenda had spent all of the time alone constructing this plan. As the other officers dispersed throughout the house to search for concrete evidence as to how she committed suicide, once again, the coroner was called to claim yet another body. It was now evident that this incident had taken on a life of its own.

Brenda had turned her bedroom into a shrine. It had been decorated with everything bridal. You could tell that she had spent several months constructing everything. Anything stationary was draped with bridal lace; and every stitch of furniture in the room was adorned with bridal tchotckes. There were photos of she and Chad in all of the picture frames, and a massive heart-shaped photo collage headboard had been constructed over the "coffin" that she was now lying in repose. In her arms she was clutching her favorite picture of the two of them together. Aunt Clara had to leave the room as she sobbed quietly to herself. It was all over for Brenda; now, maybe she could finally find some comfort and solace in the afterlife.

The lead officer conferred with Aunt Clara as to how much she knew about what had been going on in her niece's life. She spared no detail. "…Uh, Sarge, you might wanna come an' see this…" one of the officers said as he popped his head in the doorway.

As the lead officer once again rushed on his way to another uncertain discovery, he was beginning to dread his involvement in this whole investigation. It had gotten more and more complicated with each turn of event. There, tucked away in a closet in Brenda's spare bedroom, was all the evidence they needed. *"My Good Jeeeezus…!!"* Aunt Clara sighed in desperation; as she enacted the sign of the cross, for she had not prepared for the horror she'd just witnessed.

Chapter Twenty Nine

As she sat there alone; just the glowing embers of her cigarette to help illuminate the darkness, she allowed her body to succumb to the effects of the glass of warm cognac that she was nursing. Her mind began to drift and wander back over the circumstances that led her to this point in her life; events that impacted her future. Every sinew of her toned, supple and lithe body was now glistening with sweat beads as she pondered her next move. Why had she not seen all of the tell-tale signs that had lead up to that fateful night?

She was startled, a little, by the sound of the doorbell, and she wondered; Now what? Her life has certainly taken a dramatic turn within the last seventy-two hours. Once again, the lead officer was standing at her doorway, asking if he could come in. Bianca was a bit apprehensive, but graciously acquiesced. The officer told her that he was there to update her as to the outcome of the investigation, and to get some final clarification before they were able to close the case.

According to the police investigation, and in light of all of the evidence collected, it was an open-and-shut case. The victims and the perpetrator had all been accounted for. He divulged to her what she basically had already been told by several nosey on-lookers, and those who had been present to piece together all of the different scenes into a more cohesive arrangement.

It became all too clear that Brenda had been the one who initiated the chain of events, according to Aunt Clara. She had become despondent upon learning that Chad had; indeed, fallen back in love with Tyreke after all these years. Brenda had; several months prior to Bianca's party, contracted an investigator to follow Chad and get evidence of his philandering. According to the officer; Brenda at some point, became obsessed with destroying Chad and Tyreke, once she had physical proof of his infidelity. The dates on the photos also pre-dated the Christmas party Bianca threw.

Brenda had already planned on being the one that discovered them once she recognized Tyreke from the photos. Suddenly, it all became clear to Bianca...*she* had been played. Brenda had been fully aware all that time as to what was going on; *she* had putting on an act for all of them, also. When Bianca asked the officer how it was discovered that she was the killer, he told her that Brenda had also constructed an altar; only this one was one of evil, hatred and vindication. They had found the negatives to all of the pictures that she had been blackmailing them with; and she had even pasted them up on the walls of her make-shift alter. She had written post-it notes to them that they were going to pay for their sins, and had stuck them onto the pictures. They'd also found the poison that she'd used on all three of them; since warfarin was so readily available as a poison to kill rats.

To the best of their summation, once she had discovered them at the reception, something in her snapped. She came back to her house, got the poison, returned to the reception and poisoned both of their drinks just before she'd handed them off to the both of them. She made sure that her toast was long enough so that they would have to drink the whole glass. It was also the coroner's assumption that the food intake had slowed down the process of the poison from not killing them instantly; which was why they'd died at home. She must have come home; changed clothes and drank the poison herself before she climbed into bed and waited to die.

Bianca was a bit perplexed as to why she was blackmailing Caleb. According to the officer, she wasn't. She just made his life a living hell by sending him the pictures, letting him know that she knew what he was up to, just as she had done with Chad and Tyreke.

Neither of them would ever know that it all boiled down to one simple kiss in a church parking lot that sent one person on the path of destruction. They would all have to be satisfied with the findings of the coroner's inquest. No one, but Bianca, will ever know the real reason that drove Brenda to carry out such a heinous act. Bianca knew; deep in her heart, why Brenda *had* to do what she had done. There was no other recourse for her. How could she have saved face after being publicly humiliated in that way? Bianca knew- for it was Bianca; *not* Brenda, who initially set the ball in motion.

After the officer left, Bianca set about closing up the house for the evening. Her mind began to wander as she silently goes over the list of things she must do to prepare for Caleb's funeral. The list is actually a very short one; as his parents have stepped in and made all of the arrangements themselves. All that she has to do is hop on a plane, show up, shed a few tears, and *pretend* to be the grief-stricken widow. As she departs the living room, she rehearses the range of emotions she will be expected to show. She takes a few seconds to go through them all in the hallway mirror, just to make sure she's not too 'over the top'. She only has to keep this up for a few more weeks; both Leslie and Allison have postponed their honeymoons until after the funerals, and Charmaine and Randi will meet up with them in Caleb's hometown of Mobile, Alabama, on the day of his funeral.

As she makes her ascent up the staircase, Bianca chuckled to herself at the ironic chain of events. For a brief second, she questions whether or not she should feel sorry for Brenda, if no one else.

What for? I tried to warn her from the beginning about Chad, but she wouldn't listen….she got what she deserved.
And with that; she turned off the hallway light, and closed her bedroom door.
It's finally over; once and for all, she said to herself as a smile of contentment crept slowly across her face…

Finis

J. Toby McKinney

The author of several published works, including his most recent novel: "Life's Altered Path". Some of his poetry is featured in the anthology "Silence is Death: Voices United". An original facilitator with "BrothersSpeak/Broward" mentorship group; J. Toby McKinney lends his support when needed, and often serves as a guest panel facilitator at the "UJIMA Black Men's Conferences". A Gulf War veteran, he is also a member of Kappa Psi Kappa Fraternity, Inc. J. Toby McKinney is currently the Owner/Editor of **Today'sMale** blog.

Originally from Pittsburgh, PA; J. Toby is an alumnus of Grambling State University, where he received his Master's in Education. Currently he's working on completing several manuscripts, and an anthology of short stories and poems.

Other works by J. Toby McKinney:

"Innocence Lost"

"For The Love of Hip Hop"

"Life's Altered Path"

Email J.Toby McKinney:

j.tobymckinney@gmail.com

www.ingramcontent.com/pod-product-compliance
Lightning Source LLC
Chambersburg PA
CBHW051817090426

42736CB00011B/1518